FAIRS
&
FESTIVALS

ILLINOIS, INDIANA & OHIO

FAIRS & FESTIVALS

ILLINOIS, INDIANA & OHIO

SALLY McKINNEY

COUNTRY ROADS PRESS
Oaks • Pennsylvania

Published by Country Roads Press
P.O. Box 838, 2170 West Drive
Oaks, PA 19456

Text design & Typesetting by Allen Crider.
Cover Illustration by Dale Ingrid Swensson.
Illustrations by Anna Finkel.

ISBN 1-56626-134-1

Library of Congress Cataloging-in-Publication Data

McKinney, Sally.
    Fairs & festivals: Illinois, Indiana & Ohio / author, Sally
    McKinney ; illustrator, Anna Finkel.
            p.   cm.
    Includes index.
    ISBN 1-56626-134-1
    1. Festivals—Middle West.   2. Fairs—Middle West.
    3. Middle West—Social life and customs.   I. Title
GT4805.7.M35   1995
394.2'6977—dc20   95-18858
                    CIP

Printed in the United States of America.
10 9 8 7 6 5 4 3 2 1

Dedication

Behind every festival are the hundreds—even thousands—of paid workers and volunteers who work long hours to make things happen. Here's to all those great Midwest people!

Contents

September

October

November

December

Acknowledgements

Peas people in the heartland put great effort into creating, promoting, and organizing festivals. As each festival grows, it usually gets better, and the hosts have as much fun as the guests.

This book is dedicated to all the people who have worked to make the heartland fairs and festivals possible, from the history buffs behind the Lincoln Day service to the promoters and exhibitors in the huge Adventure Travel Show.

Special thanks goes as well to everyone who has made this book possible:

Rachel Munday, for example, helped build the book from blocks of words I gave her. Nan K. Smith sailed through a stack of rough pages. Lisa Duda responded overnight to my request for a list of Indiana festivals even though the booklet hadn't been printed yet. Janet Mathis rushed me all the information, leaving nothing out. Daryl Watson came through when someone else was hospitalized. Ann Frazier explained things as thoroughly as if she had all the time in the world.

Special thanks also to my sister, Judy Brown, whose descriptions made the Grant Park Symphony section come alive. My mother, Hazel Brown, kindly shared childhood recollections of the Fountain Park Chautauqua. My four grown sons—Brian, Mark,

Bruce, and Matt—have always been delightfully supportive when I write about my home region.

Additional thanks go to Noelle Sojka, Tami Parker, Mary Endsley, Deb Herman, Janice Craig, Martha Catherwood, Susan Goehring, Kathleen Crews, Edson Devore, Carolyn Mosby, Tamara Owens, Mariellen Fagan, Glennas Kueck, Dee Grossman, Judy Gregurich, Bob Buchanan, Kim Krieger, Laura Gundrum, Debby Scott, Jacquelyn Harris, and that wonderful anonymous person from Bishop Hill who fashioned an envelope from brown paper in order to send material right away.

Please be aware that much of the work of putting on festivals is done by volunteers. Moreover, the professional publicists, directors, media coordinators, and so on also donate hours of what would otherwise be their free time in support of the festivals. The people at the Indianapolis Project, Inc., for example, are so dedicated they put home phone numbers on the media contact sheet.

Finally, many thanks to the great people at Country Roads Press. Editors Margery Read, Liza Fosburgh, and publisher John White have put much effort into this book. I appreciate the effort Country Roads Press has made to encourage more travel in this region. Here, people mean it when they say, "Glad to see you."

Introduction

Indiana, Illinois, and Ohio Fairs and Festivals
by Sally McKinney

Once covered with trees and wild grasses, these three fertile states nourished by rivers and dotted with lakes share a regional history. Mound builders left behind evidence of early societies that thrived here and there in Indiana and Ohio. French explorers and adventurers who paddled through this territory in the seventeenth century found tribes of woodland Indians living with respect for the land. Buffalo, deer, smaller game, and fish that leaped from rivers and lakes inspired seasonal feasting.

During the eighteenth century, this hotly contested territory was still the Wild West—a roomy frontier land where people could settle in hopes of building something with their labors, be it an oasis of civilization, a religious community, or a business with transportation links to the Great Lakes ports.

Within this region they found wide seasonal temperature swings, geographic isolation, mysterious illnesses, tribal conflicts, and wild predators. The settlers sometimes buried their loved ones before their time. Yet those who survived learned how much work, commitment, and caring it took to make dreams into reality.

As favored modes of transport shifted from river boats on rivers to stagecoaches on roads and from canals to railroads to highways, the earliest towns flourished or stagnated. People learned to celebrate the seasonal changes. They understood that there was a time to scatter seeds and a time to harvest. They knew there would come a fallow time, and that death was part of the cycle.

The heartland's fairs and festivals are rooted in this early history. The French and Indians celebrated at autumn trade fairs. The early missionaries who came to the region brought their holiday traditions of Christmas, New Year's, and Easter from the old country. After shedding British control, newly autonomous Americans began celebrating Independence Day with flag waving and patriotic songs.

Today, the hundreds of fairs and festivals that take place throughout the year in Indiana, Ohio, and Illinois trace their roots to the values of these early days. The Feast of the Hunter's Moon, held near Lafayette, Indiana, celebrates the return of the Voyageurs from their arduous, seasonal journeys to the French outpost at Fort Ouiatenon from Montreal. The Coshocton Canal Festival, held in a restored canal town, commemorates the arrival of the first canal boat from the town of Cleveland. The harvest festival known as Jordbruksdagarna (Agriculture Days) in Bishop Hill, Illinois, pays tribute to the early founders of the community, who—having traveled much of the way from Sweden by ship—walked the last hundred and sixty miles across the prairie.

Perhaps because survival requires more of people here, children growing up in the heartland learn early what it takes to make something happen. When heartland communities put on a festival, they do so with great spirit, working together to reach their goal. At times it seems that whenever three or more people here get together, they organize a festival!

In her biography of Warren Webster (*An American Biography: An Industrialist Remembers the Twentieth Century*, [Washington, D.C.: Farragut Publishing Company, 1995, pp. 216-217]) Pat McNees provides an inside look at the way Webster helped launch the Holiday at Home Festival in Kettering, Ohio. Webster was involved with promoting YMCA memberships, and part of the idea "was to create a local festival so people would stay off the roads (where there were many fatalities each Labor Day weekend)." Webster found out that putting on a parade is a monster job: "We ended up recruiting about four hundred people to help. There's a lot of work to do for a parade. The only thing I did on these projects was to provide some leadership. The smart leaders hire someone else smart to do the job. On all these projects, a lot of people worked together." McNees explains, "As a membership-raiser, the 1958 parade was a dud, producing only one or two memberships. But the parade itself was a success. Newspapers reported a crowd of 35,000 spectators watching another three thousand marchers in two hundred units, including classic cars and six beauty contestants. Kettering's Holiday at Home Festival became an annual tradition and appears to have saved many lives."

Even now, as the twentieth century ends, people can find in Indiana, Ohio, and Illinois a dazzling array of festivals, from a winterfest held outdoors in January to a gala mistletoe ball one evening in December. There are festivals organized around persimmons, Easter, buzzards, frozen waterfalls, and James Dean's birthday. But most importantly, as the folks in Marietta, Ohio, like to say, "Come early, and stay late!"

*Bells jingle, horses stamp, and riders laugh and sing
their sleighing songs at La Porte's Winterfest.*

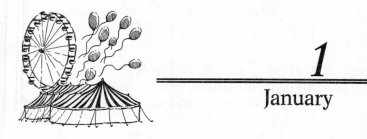

Bluegrass Music Festival
Quincy, Illinois

There's a solution to January in this part of the world: Go inside a warm place and stay there, until there's something worth coming out for. The bluegrass music fans in southern Illinois know just what that something is!

The Bluegrass Music Festival held in Quincy, Illinois, during the last weekend in January features at least half a dozen bluegrass groups from around the Midwest. The McGee Creek Connection, Sally Mountain Show, the Larkin and the Raley family groups, the River Ramblers, and Midnight Flight have all played at earlier festivals, and everybody has a great time.

Named for President John Quincy Adams, the Mississippi River town of Quincy was the place where the famous Lincoln/Douglas debate took place. Now a commercial center, the town was once the second largest in Illinois. Quincy's renovated downtown has become an historic district, and the town (population 40,000) boasts many restored Victorian homes.

The Bluegrass Music Festival takes place at the Holiday Inn which has a dining room and a heated swimming pool. Admission is charged for each performance; save by buying a weekend pass. Children under twelve are admitted to events free when accompanied by an adult. Please contact the Downstate Illinois Bluegrass Association, 217-243-3159, for exact dates and times of this and other festivals. The Holiday Inn offers a special rate for the event; call 217-222-2666 for information and reservations. The Quincy Convention and Visitors Bureau has specifics about other accommodations, restaurants, and attractions in the area. Call 800-978-4748.

Besides the festival at Quincy, the Downstate Bluegrass Association holds other festivals in different locations throughout the year. In Illinois, you can choose from a festival in Naperville in March, another held at a campground near Havana in July, the Rockome Gardens Bluegrass Festival near Arcola in August, another in Pontiac in September, and yet another in Decatur in November. **For more information, contact the Downstate Bluegrass Association at 217-243-3159.**

Winterfest

La Porte, Indiana

The northern Indiana counties along Lake Michigan's shore (Lake, Porter, and La Porte Counties) lie in a snow belt where winter provides all sorts of drama: tree limbs that fall across sidewalks, driveways that fill with snow, streets that resemble ice-skating rinks, and cars stuck in ditches. Yet at times the winter landscape can become a sparkling wonderland.

The folks who live in La Porte County don't let winter close them in. Instead, the La Porte Parks and Recreation Department hosts a month-long festival that gives people eighteen or so indoor and outdoor activities to choose from, with something for everyone in the family. These events take place at various locations in La Porte, at the county fairgrounds, and at the La Porte parks from early January into early February. Occasionally, certain events have their times or dates shifted because of weather problems, while other events go on no matter what.

The amateur ice sculptors usually display their creations around the county courthouse. They'll spend several days on these masterpieces, making anything from Noah's Ark to a Chicago Bulls symbol. In the same location, professional ice-carving teams turn out more than a dozen sculptures. Recent carvings have included a hammer and screwdriver, a swan, a duck flying out of a pond, and an eagle. One special favorite was something everyone here can relate to—a tow truck with car being towed.

Cross-country skiers bring along their equipment, and a group usually goes out for a midnight ski. The region's hardy ice fishermen compete on La Porte's many small lakes; they also hold a junior competition, and reporters from the local media handle the announcement of the winners as breaking news. The area's antiques shops host a tour in which shoppers in automobiles (hopefully, they're equipped with snow tires) follow a map of routes along country roads to the host shops in various locations.

Winterfest includes all sorts of tournaments, from a snowball volleyball tournament to a pinochle contest. Local school children take part in art-essay contests. The park department usually sponsors a bird-watching breakfast, great for the whole family. A horse-drawn sleigh rally involves competition in many different classes and is guaranteed to bring out nostalgia in anyone who's ever traveled that way. But it isn't all snow and ice. During one past Winterfest, Mermaid's Quest Scuba Boutique offered a free scuba session in a local pool.

All events are free to spectators, but some contests have an entry fee. **For more Winterfest information, call 219-326-9600 or 219-326-1945 or 219-324-5855;** you'll get a real person during the day or recorded information after hours.

The Holiday Inn/Holidome (444 Pine Lake Avenue) has a restaurant, a pool, bellhop service, a shopping arcade, and recreation and game rooms.

Tangerine (601 Michigan Avenue) serves lunch and dinner in a renovated nineteenth-century hotel building.

Call the La Porte County Convention and Visitors Bureau, 219-872-5055 or 800-634-2650, for information about other attractions.

International Adventure Travel Show

Rosemont, Illinois

Scurry down the sidewalk through Chicago's skyscraper canyons—get hit by a blast of winter wind from the lakefront—and you'll soon be fantasizing a tropical escape. Perhaps you crave a dugout canoe adventure on the Kalawari River or a sailing adventure in the Florida Keys or a bicycle tour from one inn to another in New Mexico, pedaling at your own pace by day and eating wonderful food at night.

*Fight off winter blahs with dreams of adventure—in a
warmer climate—at the International Adventure Show.*

The promoters of the International Adventure
Travel Show understand all this. That's why they
launched this show in downtown Chicago a few years

back, and that's why it's grown large enough to require a space the size of the Rosemont O'Hare Convention Center. The January or February weekend trade fair features over two hundred adventure tour operators, national and international tourism organizations, airlines, and even travel publications. Of course, most of the people there are subtly trying to sell you their products, but you can look, look, look for no extra charge beyond the admission price.

On arrival, get an exhibitor directory before doing anything; then plan meeting places and times with those in your family who like to wander off on their own. The last page in the directory organizes the exhibitors according to an "adventure index," so that you can identify all the companies offering hiking or river rafting or photography or whatever matches your interests. There's a "destination index" as well, so that people who have always wanted to go to, say, the Yucatán or Egypt or Vanuatu can find exhibitors who organize trips to and from these destinations.

Walk from one booth to the next, and you'll find it's not all that exotic. On one visit to the Adventure Travel Show, I met the couple who run Clement's Canoes trips down Sugar Creek not more than fifty miles from my home.

Keep on walking and you'll soon find that the featured trips are not all "jump-from-the-plane-and-pray" experiences either. Some of the adventures—barge cruising, whale watching, and air safaris, for example—can be done by people with only enough skills to find the seat on a barge, boat, or plane.

Some of the tours have an educational spin: art history, bird-watching, cultural expeditions, environmental education, and research expeditions are but a few. Others appeal to special groups of consumers, like the adventure trips for singles or for women only or for women over thirty.

"Adventure travel is putting the goosebumps back in the travel business," claimed a travel agent from Ohio. She's one who came for the Friday seminar designed especially for travel agents, a session that attracted four hundred and fifty-five other travel agents before the 1995 Adventure Travel Show.

The destinations represented run the gamut from Alaska to Vanuatu—maybe they'll feature Zimbabwe next time. You can go up and talk to outfitters who'll organize a dogsled trip for you so you can play explorer in Canada's Northwest Territories, or you can learn about family programs at the Crow Canyon Archaeological Center or find out what goes on at a jungle spa in Belize.

Admission is charged. **For more information write to One Westminster Place, Lake Forest, Illinois, 60045-1821, or call 708-295-4444.**

For accommodations you can choose from hotels and motels in the O'Hare Airport area at a range of prices. Nearby restaurants are located in Rosemont or Des Plaines. For more information, contact the Chicago Office of Tourism at 312-744-2400 or 800-487-2446.

Chili Open Winter Fun Golf Classic
Catawba Island, Ohio

Many golf players claim they'll play the game any-where, any time. In January on Catawba Island, golfers get a chance to put their swings to the test when they play in a tournament with snowbanks as hazards. At the Chili Open Winter Fun Golf Classic, expect the green to be white with snow. Players hit their balls around a nine-hole par-3 course in a rugged field, hoping their efforts will merit prizes.

It's all great fun, especially warming up in a heated circus tent while the hardy players swap stories. With live entertainment, door prizes, and games of skill and chance, there is something for everyone. **For more information, contact Ottawa County Visitors Bureau at 419-743-4386 or 800-441-1271.**

Hocking Hills Winter Hike
Hocking Hills State Park, Logan, Ohio

It's the middle of January, and your wealthy friends are lying in the sun somewhere, scribbling sweaty messages onto cards that will arrive postmarked Miami or Majorca or Montego Bay.

Never mind. Pack up your boots and parkas, make your way to southeast Ohio, and forget—for a while at least—your boredom, the seasonal restless-ness, and that stack of Christmas bills.

It won't cost much to join thousands of others for the Hocking Hills Winter Hike on a winter Satur-day. For a fresh perspective shift your attention to the

Indians, the settlers, and the travelers who once followed this same trail through dense forest and
past rocky cliffs, peering into caves, winding through
a ravine, and standing in awe before the same ice-
crusted waterfalls.

During the hike, refreshments and lunch are
served, and a shuttle is provided between the parking
area and the trail. There is no charge, but a donation
is recommended. **Call Steve Bennett at 614-385-6841
for more information about the hike.** Call Hocking
County tourism, 800-HOCKING, for places to stay
and to dine and for other area attractions.

Winter Wilderness Weekend

Starved Rock State Park, Utica, Illinois

S tarved Rock, a sandstone butte beside the Illinois
River, was the site of an early French fort. Go for
the Winter Wilderness Weekend in January, and guides
will take you to see the spectacular ice falls. Cross-
country skiing instruction and equipment are also
available.

The park has fifteen miles of hiking trails and
bluffs and canyons formed centuries ago by melting
glaciers. Come back in spring (early May) when the
wildflowers peak, to discover more than two hundred
different kinds of flowers.

The park has a lodge, a visitors center, and a
restaurant. **Call 815-667-4906 for more information.**

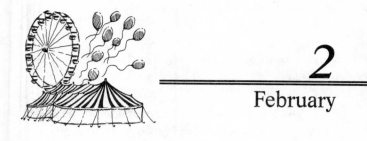

2
February

James Dean Birthday Celebration
Fairmount, Indiana

This event may rank among the region's smallest, but that's not important. People come from all across the country to celebrate the birthday of a boy who grew up here and became a film star. Each year in February, on or near James Dean's birthday, people who remember him gather in Fairmount, Indiana, to watch one of his films, eat some cake, and maybe wonder about the meaning of an interrupted life.

The James Dean Birthday Celebration is not very structured. People wander around looking at James Dean memorabilia and at his old high-school building. Some visitors attend a dinner dance on Saturday night. One of Dean's films is usually shown on Sunday, and then there's the birthday cake shared with other fans.

James Dean, the actor whose *East of Eden* and *Rebel Without a Cause* have become film classics, was born on February 8, 1931. He died in California in an automobile accident on September 30, 1955. Had he gone on living, he would have celebrated his 65th birthday in 1996.

His hometown hasn't grown much over the years, so it's easy to find Dean's grave at Park Cemetery, the Old Fairmount High School on Vine Street, and the legendary motorcycle shop he frequented as a teenager.

The Fairmount Historical Museum on the corner of Walnut and Washington houses an exhibit of James Dean memorabilia and personal items. It's here that you'll see the motorcycles he owned, his racing suit, still photogaphs, and artwork. Additional displays honor Jim Davis, creator of the "Garfield" cartoons, and two other natives. (Donation suggested.)

The James Dean Gallery and Gift Shop (425 Main Street) claims to have the world's largest collection of James Dean memorabilia. Here you can contemplate the clothing he wore in his films, his high-school yearbooks, and a rare Warner Brothers life mask, along with movie posters, books, magazines, and so on. The gift shop sells nostalgic souvenirs. (Admission charge.) The museum and gallery both remain open throughout the James Dean celebration.

The James Dean birthday dance sponsored by the Memories Diner during past festivals, follows a 1950's theme. Expect a sock hop (shoes are left at the door to prevent scuffing the floor of the gym where these dances are held), complete with bobby socks, "New Look" skirts, and maybe even ducktails (boys' haircuts with tails). What's more, as with typical high-school dances of that period, there's no alcohol being drunk here—at least, not within sight of other people.

Sunday brings a special showing (usually in the municipal building) of a classic James Dean film. Afterward, meet some Fairmount residents over punch or coffee and share their memories. In a small town like this, residents once knew almost everyone, and the older ones remember the legendary film star as one of many youngsters growing up here. For the last few years, Carla Smith has been baking the James Dean birthday cake and decorating it with flowers. Smith isn't from Fairmount, but her family is, and they remember James Dean well.

"My mother rode the school bus with him," she confides, "and my husband's mother knew his aunt . . . they went to the same church."

That's how it is in small town Indiana.

The James Dean Birthday Celebration takes place on Saturday and Sunday of the first weekend in February. Fairmount, where the events are held, is five miles west of the State 26 exit from I-69, the interstate that links Indianapolis and Fort Wayne. Usually about a hundred dedicated James Dean fans attend. **Contact the Fairmount Historical Museum, 317-948-4555, for festival and museum information.** Contact the James Dean Gallery, 317-948-3326, for information about the dinner dance.

Note that the community also hosts a major festival called Fairmount Museum Days: Remembering James Dean during the last full weekend in September. Call the Marion/Grant County Convention and Visitors Bureau, 800-662-9474 or 317-668-5435, for more information about this event.

Nearby Marion has several motels and inns. The Holiday Inn usually offers a James Dean Birthday Celebration package that includes a welcome gift, dinner for two, lodging, gallery admission, breakfast, the party, and the screening, all for a special rate. Call 317-668-8801 for more information.

The Memories Diner usually offers a James Dean dinner special before the dance.

Contact Marion/Grant County Convention and Visitors Bureau, 800-662-9474 or 317-668-5435, for more information about lodging, dining, and attractions in the area.

Lincoln Day Observance
Evansville, Indiana

The annual Lincoln Day Observance—a memorial service that dates back to 1924—takes place at the Lincoln Boyhood National Memorial about thirty miles northeast of Evansville. Held on the Sunday nearest February 12, the day the legendary president was born, the memorial program involves a speech, patriotic music, and remarks by important guests. After the program, those gathered proceed to the grave of Lincoln's mother, Nancy Hanks Lincoln, who died when Lincoln was nine years old. A eulogy and wreath-laying cermony are followed by refreshments. **For more information, call 812-937-4541.**

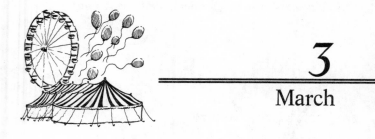

3
March

Parke County Maple Fair
Parke County, Indiana

Like most of Indiana, the terrain of Parke County was at one time forested. The Illinois, Huron, and Miami Indians hunted this land broken by steep cliffs, gorges, and bubbling streams. While early settlers forded the streams, those who came later built covered bridges. Today, thirty-three of these early wooden structures remain in Parke County; neighboring Putnam County has ten more. Although the autumn Covered Bridge Festival has a larger attendance, the Parke County Maple Fair is equally fascinating.

Held each year during the last weekend in February and the first weekend in March, the Parke County Maple Fair, with headquarters in Rockville at the county fairgrounds, involves tours of half a dozen maple syrup camps found along the same back roads that link the covered bridges. At these camps you can watch maple syrup and maple candies being made on working Indiana farms. Back at the fairgrounds you can enjoy real maple syrup, fresh pancakes, and tasty regional dishes.

In early spring, warm days followed by cold nights cause the sap to rise in maple trees. Farmers use spigots driven into holes bored in the tree trunks to funnel the sap into buckets. They make maple syrup by boiling down the sap of the sugar- or rock-maple

How sweet it is at the Indiana maple sugar fairs.

tree. Generally it takes 32 to 35 gallons (121–132 liters) of maple sap to produce one gallon of maple syrup. Evaporated maple syrup becomes maple sugar.

Some Native Americans made syrup from sap tapped through hollow reeds. Using pails and rough-hewn log troughs, the colonists likewise collected the sap, then boiled it in kettles hung over cooking fires on poles.

Begin your trip to the Parke County Maple Fair by checking in at the 4-H fairgrounds (one mile north of Rockville on US 41) to get a map showing the routes to the maple camps. If you'd rather not drive yourself, they have buses that tour the camps.

Between the scenic drives to see maple farms, explore the fairgrounds. The Commercial Building holds the Home Folks' Market featuring handicrafts, baked goods, and canned preserves and jellies. In the Butcher Shop they sell the smoked hams, bacon, and sausages used in so many regional dishes. The pancake, sausage, and maple-syrup breakfast is served until 4:00 p.m.

If it's maple sweets you're after, head for the 4-H Building, where the maple syrup producers have booths, samples of their products, and brochures. They are also very interesting people to talk to. The art association is here too, as are the china painters, who are not from China; they paint designs on china plates and platters.

During this maple fair, there's also a maple fair at Billie Creek Village (just east of Rockville on State 36). The special attraction is the primitive sugar camp in action. The pioneer syrup-makers use the old oaken buckets, spoons, and troughs, and boil the syrup over log fires.

While you're there, wander about the buildings clustered beside a stream and peek into the old covered bridges on the Billie Creek grounds.

Children will enjoy getting out to explore Billie Creek Village. The thirty or so historic buildings are linked by wooden walkways. Compare the old school house—where several grades were taught in the same room—with modern facilities. A ride in a rickety hay wagon pulled by horses makes a great finale.

Some of these area farmers have been making maple syrup for generations, and they're still family operations. One summer I saw a sign for the Williams and Teague family farm and turned off the highway. They had only a few half-pints of syrup left, and I bought some in a tiny log cabin can.

Indiana farmers are major hog producers, so pork in all its incarnations—fresh and cured—is found in many dishes: ham and beans, pork chops and scalloped potatoes, and even BLT's. At the farm-style spread offered during the maple fair, you'll find ham sandwiches, baked beans (often made with bits of ham), coleslaw (the vitamin C in cabbage helped farm families get through the long winter), and drinks like apple cider (made with apples from the farmer's own fruit trees). The Maple Fair and other harvest festivals held throughout the Midwest celebrate the bounty of this region.

You're sure to find a souvenir you like made by local craftspeople. Take home some maple syrup, of course, or maybe a few maple-sugar candies. Perhaps you'd prefer a book of local recipes, a painting of a covered bridge, or a photograph of the Mansfield Mill

If time is short, you don't need to visit all the maple camps to see how it's done. Go out to just one or two camps, then spend the rest of the time seeing the bridges. The Parke County Convention and Visitors Bureau has a map of them all. If I were to choose one favorite route among the five, I'd take the black route, which is thirty-eight miles long and includes six covered bridges. The village of Bridgeton with its impressive bridge is charming. The Mansfield Roller Mill—the best example of transitional mill technology in the state—has been placed on the National Register of Historic Places. There's also an 1878 vintage house, a country store, and a crafts shop in Parke County. The route ends conveniently at the re-created (and more commercial) Billie Creek Village.

Admission is free to the Parke County Maple Fair, but admission is charged for Billie Creek Village. The Maple Trail leading to the camps where syrup is made runs north and east of Rockville through rural Parke County.

Book your accommodations ahead. You can stay in Suits Us Bed and Breakfast on College Street in Rockville or at one of several local motels. The Parke County Convention and Visitors Bureau operates an In-Home Housing program throughout the year. They charge a $5.00 booking fee, and guests may choose either a town or farm home. For more information on this program, call 317-569-5226.

Rockville is also the county seat. Stroll around the town square to admire the Second Empire courthouse. Many of the nineteenth-century Italianate shop buildings have been restored. The G & M Variety Store (the owners are Gary and Mary) will remind you of an old dime store. This one stocks more than eight thousand items, everything from artificial flowers to live pets. On the north side of the square, the local art association operates a gallery.

On the east side of the square is the Parke Cafe. When I first wandered inside it and discovered pleasant people, local food, and not a tourist in sight, I knew I was in small-town Indiana. At 102 East Ohio Street in Rockville there's an old-time soda shop. Go three blocks farther east to 411 East Ohio (also State 36) and you'll find the Rockville Antique Mall, where glassware, furniture, primitives, and collectibles are sold by fifteen different dealers. Call 317-569-6873 for days and hours.

A nearby attraction is Turkey Run State Park, the entrance to which is located north of Rockville via State 41, then east two miles on State 47. One of Indiana's most scenic state parks, Turkey Run spans Sugar Creek. There are ten hiking trails ranging from easy to rugged, picnic shelters, a nature center, cabins, and a campground. The Turkey Run Inn provides lodging and a restaurant. Both the park and the inn are open year-round.

Seventeen miles west of Rockville on State 36 lies the town of Dana. This tiny burg in the middle of prairie farmer country is known now as the boyhood home of the famed World War II correspondent Ernie Pyle. The 1894 Victorian Castle Bed and Breakfast offers convenient lodging.

For more information about the Parke County Maple Fair, lodging, and attractions, call the Parke County Convention and Visitors Center at

317-569-5226. For more information about the Maple Fair at Billie Creek Village, call 317-567-3430.

Other Maple Sugar Fairs in Indiana

The Maple Sugarbush Festival takes place in Evansville, Indiana, at the Wesselman Woods Nature Preserve on the first weekend in March. The program involves a slide show, a guided hike, and observation of syrup-making at the sugar shed. On Saturday, come hungry for the pancake breakfast. (Admission charge.) Call 812-479-0771 for more information.

Maple Sugar Time at Deep River County Park/Woods Mill near Merrillville, Indiana, heralds spring on the first and second weekend in March. At this festive educational event you can tour the operation to learn how it works, see movies, watch the gristmill, listen to interpreters, taste pure maple syrup, and buy maple-sugar candy. (Free admission.) Call 219-769-7275 for more information.

Also held on the first and second weekends in March, the Maple Sugar Festival at Chellberg Farm/Bailly Homestead (part of the Indiana Dunes National Lakeshore) involves demonstrations of both pioneer and modern syrup-making methods. Tours begin every ten minutes, and live music adds to the fun. **Call 219-926-7561 for more information.**

Buzzard Day
Hinckley Township, Ohio

Capistrano has its swallows, the Platte River Valley has its sandhill cranes, and then there's Hinckley Township, Ohio. Old-timers recall how the buzzards have always returned to Hinckley Township on March 15 each year to nest in the hollow logs, stumps, and dense shrubbery of a lakeside reserve in Hinckley's southeast corner.

Each year since 1958, residents of this suburban area south of Cleveland have celebrated the return of the buzzards—which are actually turkey vultures (Cathartes aura)—on the Sunday following their mid-March arrival. The festival takes place in the Hinckley Elementary School, as well as at the Buzzard Roost area of the 2,500-acre Hinckley Reservation, one of a dozen parks in the Cleveland Metroparks system.

The good people of Hinckley saw a need for this community effort after the word about the buzzards spread rapidly in 1957. One month in advance, a Cleveland newspaper reporter aroused the interest of naturalists, ornithologists, and a curious public by predicting the date of the birds' arrival. The nine thousand or so visitors who descended on the community—field glasses in hand—nearly overwhelmed the township's ability to provide sustenance and shelter.

Now, the township prepares for the influx of visitors with a regularity that rivals the buzzards' timing. The Chamber of Commerce launches Buzzard Day with a pancake-and-sausage breakfast on the Sunday following the fifteenth of March. Visitors pay one price for sausage, juice, milk, a hot beverage, and all the pancakes they can eat. Children and "seasoned citizens" get special lower rates. The festive meal takes place in the school, where guests can make the acquaintance of a buzzard named Gawk.

Sometimes called a flying garbage can, the buzzard performs an important ecological function by feeding on carrion. Weighing four or five pounds, with a wingspan of up to six feet, the bird will ride thermals and updrafts in order to locate the dead raccoons, possums, skunks, snakes, turtles, frogs, and fish that make up its diet. Gregarious and downright ugly, the birds will gather on a dead tree by the dozens.

One good place to see them is at Buzzard Roost, near a picnic area that can be reached via West Drive into the Hinckley Reservation. On Buzzard Sunday, naturalists and park rangers hover nearby, ready to share their stories about the birds and to answer all your questions, such as when did the birds start coming? Why do they come back? How do they know when to come? Why do they come to Hinckley?

An early manuscript by William Coggswell, one of the first white visitors to explore the area, mentions sighting "vultures of the air" near the place by the Rocky River where Wyandot Indians had hanged a squaw for witchcraft. A few years later, several hundred hunters in the area held a "great Hinckley varmint hunt" just before Christmas in order to eliminate many of the predators—especially wolves, bears, and foxes—that were killing the hogs, sheep, and other animals they were trying to raise. The carrion left from this large-scale slaughter would have been very appealing to the turkey vultures.

Although some vultures migrate to South America, others winter in Kentucky, Tennessee, and Virginia. One theory is that the increase in daylight triggers their return to summer range. The Hinckley Reserve, with its limited human use and combination of rocky ledges, woodlands, open fields, and lake provides the kind of habitat the birds need for nesting, tending their young, and hunting for carrion.

Adults will enjoy shopping for hand-crafted items and souvenirs of Buzzard Day; children will enjoy the special games and the DJ who provides music; and everyone will enjoy the hospitality of a community that makes visitors—and buzzards—welcome.

Souvenirs of the event are much sought after and can be obtained throughout the year from the festival sponsors. **For more information contact the Hinckley Chamber of Commerce, PO Box 354, Hinckley, OH 44233; 216-278-2066.**

There is no admission fee. About three thousand people attend the breakfast, and many more go to see the dozens of buzzards in the park. Hinckley Township can be reached via I-71, which runs south of the Cleveland airport. Exit onto State 303 (also called Center Road) and continue east to State 44. Turn south and cross Bellus Road to enter Hinckley Reserve. Pass East Drive and turn right onto West Drive in order to view the buzzards.

The Cleveland Metropolitan Area has many lodging options, including several Harley Hotels, Holiday Inns, and Days Inns. Glidden House—conveniently located near the art museum, the natural history museum, and other attractions—is a European-style

inn with several dozen rooms and suites
(216-231-8900).

While you're in the area, don't miss the Cleveland Metroparks Zoo (3900 Brookside Park Drive),
which showcases more than thirty-three hundred animals on a 165-acre wooded site. The glass-roofed Rain
Forest houses several hundred animals and some ten
thousand plants in a moist, steamy environment.
(Admission charge.)

The Cleveland Museum of Art (11150 East
Boulevard, University Circle) has a permanent collection ranked among the top five in the nation. Admission is free, but there is a charge for special exhibits.

For more information about Cleveland lodging,
dining, and attractions, call 800-321-1004.

Celebrate spring with the Floral Festival in Cincinnati.

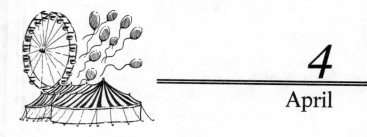

Mansfield Mushroom Festival

Mansfield, Indiana

Way back when Midwesterners couldn't buy entertainment, parents and children had to think up
things to do. Winter vacations, weekends, and holidays
all meant time to be filled. When spring came at last,
parents and kids alike would use any excuse to get
outside, and one of the great spring outings was a
mushroom hunt. While tramping through the woods,
everyone's hopes focused on the elusive morel mushrooms they hoped to find along the path ahead.

In Parke County, Indiana, they still hunt mushrooms. They even hold a yearly festival—the Mansfield
Mushroom Festival—on the last full weekend in April.
The event takes place in the village of Mansfield,
where there's a lovely old mill reflected in the pond.

Each Saturday and Sunday of the festival, the
main activity is a mushroom hunt for all ages. Participants must pay a fee and register between 8:00 and
10:00 A.M.; then they take off into the woods to search
for the elusive fungi. There's a limit of one hundred
entrants, and the winners in various categories receive
prizes when the hunt is over.

Each day there's also a mushroom contest in
which people enter the biggest mushrooms they can
find anywhere in the hope of winning one of the cash

prizes. On both days, there's a mushroom auction; it's usually held between 10:00 A.M. and 12:00 noon, and from 1:00 to 3:00 P.M. Buyers and sellers come from all over, and the excitement is something to see.

Food booths have mushrooms to eat, along with other homegrown and homemade edibles, and additional booths are set up to sell crafts, antiques, and white elephants.

To reach Mansfield, take US 36 west from Indianapolis, drive six miles south on State 39, and turn in at Mansfield. **Call 317-653-4026 or 317-653-4782 for more information.**

Easter Sunrise Service
Schoenbrunn, Ohio

The early settlers who pushed west of the Alleghenies brought along much more than trunks of clothing and barrels of food. They also carried with them time-worn traditions of food, work, and worship, traditions rooted in the countries they left behind.

An important part of the Moravian religious tradition involves gathering at dawn on Easter morning to worship, a custom that began in Germany in the 1730s. When Moravian missionaries—aided by Christian Indians—built a settlement at Schoenbrunn in 1772, they continued the Easter sunrise service with hymns, readings, and prayers.

The Ohio Historical Society, supported by Moravian congregations in the Tuscarawas Valley, still holds a traditional Easter Sunrise Service each year at

Schoenbrunn village two miles east of New Philadelphia. Note that shifting dates make Easter a movable
feast, and the time of dawn also varies from year
to year.

Visitors gather outside the reconstructed early
meeting house, a log building that was also used as a
social center. If it rains, everyone takes the program
booklets inside, where there are wooden benches.
Words and music to the ancient hymns are printed in
each booklet, as are the creeds, responses, and prayers.
A brass choir accompanies the singing, and the service
is in English. The service concludes with a silent procession to the early cemetery on the site, where forty-
four Indian converts to Christianity were buried during
the late eighteenth century. Now surrounded by a log
fence, with flat stones marking each plot, the cemetery
was known to the early Moravians as God's Acre.

Before or after the service, visitors may wander
around the village to see the early school, the congregational garden, and a few reconstructed cabins.
There's also a trading post and a museum where
exhibits explain the complex, tragic history of the
German missionaries and their fellow Christians, the
converted Delawares. Caught in the rising tensions
between British soldiers, American rebels, and
marauding Indian tribes in the 1780s, these Indian
converts—who were in fact pacifists—were presumed
to be spies. Ultimately, ninety-six of the Christian
Indians were executed by American militia at nearby
Gnadenhutten in 1872.

**Admission to the service is free; contact Schoen-
brunn Village at 216-339-3636 for more information.**
New Philadelphia has a Days Inn, Best Western, and

Travelodge. The Atwood Lake resort near Dellroy—set on 1,540 wooded, lakeside acres—has over one hundred guest rooms, large cottages with kitchens, restaurant, and various bicycles, sailboats, tennis courts, and other recreational options. For information on dining, call the Tuscarawas County Convention and Visitors Bureau (800-527-3387).

Spring Floral Festival
Cincinnati, Ohio

In a hurry for spring? At the Cincinnati Zoo's Spring Floral Festival, held from mid-April through mid-May, you can walk through artful gardens where more than half a million bulbs bloom and thousands of blossoms burst from the branches of flowering shrubs. On the zoo grounds lilacs, magnolias, viburnums, and other trees display their spring colors too. Each weekend during this month-long festival, opera, symphony, and dance ensembles perform. (Admission charge.) **Contact the Cincinnati Zoo and Botanical Garden at 800-599-HIPPO or 513-281-4701.**

EarthFest
Crown Point, Indiana

EarthFest, a local celebration held in conjunction with the national Earth Day, allows people in northwestern Indiana to celebrate their ties to one another and their concern for life on earth. The festival involves musical entertainment, seminars, hands-on workshops, exhibits, games, contests, food, and merchandise.

Sponsored by the Lake County Solid Waste Management District, this unique festival has been planned with the entire family in mind. Past festivals have featured a play called Earth Awakenings, seminars and workshops on composting, alternatives to hazardous household waste, and a hazardous household-waste collection site. The children's building houses Ronald McDonald and his Ecology Show, science projects that will help the environment, an old-toy exchange, and so forth. The Enviromobile features even more hands-on science projects.

Food booths are designed to minimize trash and use recycled materials. Families can also enter a contest in which they try to pack a picnic in an environmentally friendly way, perhaps using plates from home instead of disposable ones.

EarthFest takes place at the Lake County Fairgrounds in Crown Point, Indiana, each April, and there is no admission charge. **Call 219-769-3820 for festival information.** Call 800-ALL-LAKE for information about lodging, dining, and attractions in Lake County.

Hot-air balloons drop in for the May Balloon Classic.

Indianapolis 500 Festival
Indianapolis, Indiana

From the first drone of low-slung race cars zooming around the Speedway track to the festive victory dinner held on Monday evening after the race, May is the time, and Indy is the place. During this month, Indianapolis, the largest city in Indiana, appears at its best. Leafy trees shade neighborhood walks in Broad-Ripple and Woodruff Place. Warm days allow you to shed a blazer, yet not get too warm. Black-and-white checked flags—the traditional signal into the winner's circle at the famous 500 mile race—decorate the twelfth-largest American city.

Many friendly people—including several thousand volunteers—work to make the Indianapolis 500 Festival a success. When it began in the late 1950s, highlights included the parade, a governor's ball, a memorial service, and a community dance on Monument Circle. By 1962, the 500 Festival Associates, Inc. (a private, non-profit organization) had taken over the coordination of festival events; since then it has grown into an area-wide, month-long celebration.

The best time of all is Memorial Day weekend, when several major events take place during one three-day period. Just before noon on the day before the race, the Delco Electronics 500 Festival Parade follows a two-mile route through downtown Indianapolis.

Parade-goers who arrive early (a good idea) enjoy patriotic music played by the Indianapolis Symphony and broadcast over a sound system. Dozens of units, floats, marching bands, costumed performers, and helium balloons make their way from Monument Circle at city center to the end. The 500 Festival princesses wave to the crowd, and celebrities smile. Drums beat, horns blare, bright balloons rise up into the sky, and confetti drifts down to the ground. Spectators fill some fifty thousand seats along the way or jostle for standing room along the route. Clowns, dancers, acrobats, police officers—participants come from every segment of the community. As a grand finale, the thirty-three race drivers and their families pass by in fancy cars. Three cars wide and eleven rows long, the parade of drivers rolls along in the year's pole positions. In all, some 150,000 spectators line the route to see what has become America's second largest parade. Now televised worldwide, the event reaches an estimated thirty million viewers.

On Saturday evening, the Indianapolis Symphony Orchestra gives a patriotic pops concert in the renovated Circle Theater in downtown Indianapolis. Another evening event is the May Balloon Classic held at Connor Prairie, an open-air living-history museum about ten miles northeast of the city center at 13400 Allisonville Road. On Saturday and Sunday evening of Memorial Day weekend, thirty-three hot- air balloons, one for each race driver, compete in a "hound-and-hare" race, with balloonists trying to follow the lead balloon as in a hunt. Guests who pay admission to the museum often bring picnic supplies, lawn chairs, and blankets for comfortable viewing of the balloons.

Many different kinds of entertainment are included in CheckerFest at Union Station. Actually a series of festive, race-inspired events held throughout the month of May, CheckerFest offers live music, contests, shows, and other activities in the renovated train station. Located southwest of Monument Circle, Union Station also boasts more than a hundred restaurants and stores. (No admission charge.)

The festival activities culminate in the Indianapolis 500 Mile Race, the world's largest one-day sporting event, held at the Speedway oval. It took Ray Harroun six hours, forty-two minutes, and eight seconds to win the first 500 race in 1911. Today, the top Indy drivers go 240 mph along the straightaways, and thousands of reporters and photographers from thirty different countries watch the heated contest.

Reserved seats for the race usually sell out months before the event. At the renovated Speedway oval, the old back straightaway bleachers for general admission ticket-holders have been replaced with spectator mounds. Note that one of these is a Family Area (no alcohol) mound at the exit of turn two. This policy creates a small island of relative sanity for families with children.

The Flag Room Lounge at the Speedway Motel next to the track could be the best place for adults to enjoy a drink. Filled with 500 Mile Race memorabilia, it's popular with the racing community. You can learn more about past 500-mile races at the nearby Indianapolis Motor Speedway Hall of Fame Museum (4790 West 16th Street, Speedway).

Eating well during the parade or the balloon classic or during the race itself is a challenge, as the available food is not very healthful. Some corporate organizers have their company guests driven to the race in limousines and provide them with gourmet box lunches. If you're footing the bill yourself, you'd do well to fortify everyone on race day with a good breakfast at your hotel or LePeep or the Original Pancake House. Then get a cooler, find a deli, and organize a noontime meal. Fried chicken is traditional, and marinated vegetable salads travel well. In Indianapolis, O'Malia's markets offer good deli breads, fresh fruits, and unforgettable brownies.

If you're looking for souvenirs, Victory Lane at Union Station specializes in race-related items. One choice might be tiny, three-quarter-inch metal replicas of Indy race cars. Get one or two cars for a few dollars each or purchase the entire starting field of thirty-three Indy racers. Another option is artist Tony Alamo's hand-painted jeans jackets honoring the Indianapolis 500. If you still haven't found anything by the time you have to leave, allow some time to go through the shops at Indianapolis International Airport. Here, you can grab a mug or a book or a big checkered flag on your way to the gate.

As a native Hoosier, I've had three different experiences with the 500 festivities, each one great in its own way. While I was working to put my then husband through medical school, we lived in the town of Speedway, and the 500 race was a splurge. Later, as guests of an architectural firm, we had VIP treatment: a driver, box seats with great views, cold drinks placed in our hands, and lunch that came gift-wrapped. Over the years our four sons grew to love racing.

Much later, with some of them married and all of us working hard, we rented motel rooms in Rensselaer, which is located beyond the blackout zone (in which the live telecast is not permitted). Sprawled on the beds, munching the goodies we'd brought along, we tracked the front-runners during every lap and had a great time. However you watch it, the Indy 500 is one of the two greatest spectacles in racing. (The other is the Brickyard 400, a NASCAR event held at the same track in August.)

For more information about the 500 Festival, contact 500 Festival Associates, Inc. at 317-636-4556. Since more than 150,000 spectators usually attend the 500 Festival Parade, you may want to purchase tickets for reserved seats through Ticketmaster (317-239-5151). Celebrity visitors include people like Paul Newman, Jane Pauley, David Letterman, plus many former race winners.

Indianapolis boasts one hundred and five hotels and restaurants that range from Peter's (sophisticated regional cuisine, 317-465-1155) to Acapulco Joe's (a favorite hole-in-the-wall, 317-637-5160). Check the May issue of Indianapolis Monthly magazine for current favorites. Special editions of the Indianapolis Star/News contain much useful race information. In addition, the Indianapolis City Center (Pan American Plaza, 201 South Capitol Avenue, Indianapolis, IN 46225, 317-237-5206 or 800-468-INDY) has information on dining, lodging, and city attractions.

While you're in Indianapolis, visit the award-winning Children's Museum, the world's largest. Its five levels contain more than 140,000 artifacts organized in ten main galleries. Most of the exhibits are educational, interactive, and fun! Call the museum at 317-924-5431.

The City Market, established in 1886, has never been out of business. Now on the National Register of Historic Places, the city market has indoor stands selling fresh produce and specialty foods, along with about twenty ethnic eateries.

At Connor Prairie, an award-winning living-history museum with a spread of several dozen historic buildings, you'll find an entire Indiana village as it might have been in 1836. Costumed actors speak to you as if you, too, are back in the nineteenth century. The phone number is 317-776-6000 or 800-966-1836.

The Eiteljorg Museum (317-636-WEST) houses an impressive collection of American Indian and Western Art in a striking adobe building. The Indianapolis Museum of Art (317-923-1330) houses important collections of neo-Impressionists, Old Masters, and oriental art. On their hundred-and-fifty-two-acre wooded grounds overlooking the White River you'll find botanical gardens, a greenhouse, a horticultural center, a restaurant, a theater, and nature trails.

The Indianapolis Zoo, built on a sixty-four-acre site in White River State Park, has one of the world's largest enclosed whale and dolphin pavilions, as well as over two thousand animals in simulated natural habitats. Living Deserts of the World exhibits myriad plants and animals under an eighty-foot geodesic dome. Call the zoo at 317-634-4567.

The historic Walker Theater, now part of the Madame Walker Urban Life Center, was once the site of performances by Louis Armstrong, Dinah Washington, and Lena Horne; it is still used for plays, concerts, and movies. The phone number is 317-236-2099.

For more Indianapolis information, call 317-639-4282 or 800-468-INDY.

500 Festival Kids' Day
Indianapolis, Indiana

Held at Monument Circle in the heart of the city, Kids' Day is part of the month-long 500 Festival celebration in Indianapolis. This free event gives kids a chance to "start" their Big Wheels "engines," make arts and crafts, play games, spread tempera paint on old cars, even learn something about fire safety—all part of the fun. Children compete for more than twelve thousand prizes at what has become the city's largest outdoor children's festival. **Call Indy Festivals, Inc. (317-636-4556) for more information.**

International Carillon Festival
Springfield, Illinois

The music made by the ringing of bells wafts down from a twelve-story tower set among the gardens of Washington Park, in the southwest part of Springfield, accessible via South Grand Avenue. The open tower of the structure holds sixty-six bronze bells with a range of five-and-a-half octaves. Together the bells weigh 73,953 pounds.

The annual International Carillon Festival, held by the Springfield Park District each May or June, features a week of recitals by the world's best carillonneurs. They play classics, folk songs, spirituals, hymns, and popular songs adapted for the bells, along with exciting new works written especially for carillon. Since it began in 1961, the International Carillon Festival has become the best-known carillon festival in the world.

The central event of the festival is a series of evening concerts by visiting carillonneurs from San Antonio, Texas; Berkeley, California; Hartford, Connecticut; and from Belgium, the Netherlands, and other countries. Each guest recitalist plays on a keyboard in the carillonneur's cabin in the tower. On a typical evening, different musicians perform at 6:00 P.M., 7:15 P.M., and 8:00 P.M. The audience can listen from a spot near the bell tower or wander around the park listening to the lovely tones of the bells.

Because of the public nature of carillon music and the fact that any unintended dissonance can be heard for miles around, carillonneurs must play very well. Some of the best carillonneurs in the world have entertained the audience during the past festivals. One of them was Bob Van Wely, an architectural engineer who regularly plays carillon for two cities in the Netherlands. He provided music by Bach and Wim Franken, along with music he wrote especially for carillon.

George Gregory, winner of an award for Distinguished Service to the Carillon, played selections that ranged from Poe Suite—The Bells (inspired by Edgar Allen Poe's poem) to the spiritual "Kumbaya."

Bernard Winsemius, carillonneur in Haarlem, the Netherlands, has played works by Debussy, Saint-Saëns, and Ravel at festivals. Winsemius, winner of the Prix d'excellence for his performances, has also made several recordings.

Philadelphia-based Janet S. Dundore has played selections by composers ranging from Martin Luther to Rodgers and Hammerstein. A performer and teacher, Dundore once played during a visit by Queen Beatrix of the Netherlands to Curacao.

Karl Keldermans, carillonneur at the Rees Memorial Carillon, has performed classical compositions by Mozart, Strauss, and Clementi, as well as his own compositions for carillon.

The musical art of the carillon goes back to bell music performed by the Chinese around two thousand years ago. In Europe during the Middle Ages, bells were hung from towers. In Belgium and the Netherlands, bells were used to strike the hour and occasionally to warn people of danger.

At the beginning of the twentieth century, the art of bell-casting revived in Europe, allowing the carillon to become a concert instrument in locations world-wide. Today, there is a Guild of Carillonneurs in North America, and twentieth-century North American composers like Emilieu Allard and Ronald Barnes are writing carillon music.

During past festivals, twenty-five to thirty-five dancers from the Springfield Ballet Company have performed in the evening on the opening and closing Sundays of the festival. The dancers move to music as varied as Scott Joplin, Vivaldi, and Patsy Cline. Mid-week there's usually a Carillon Festival banquet, and on Friday bursts of fireworks add dramatic visual effects to the musical experience.

When the carillonneurs aren't playing, take a tour of the Rees Memorial Carillon tower. During the summer, tours are given daily between noon and 8:00 P.M. Visitors can watch the carillonneurs at the keyboard, examine the bells' playing mechanisms from three different viewing decks, and even touch some of the large bells. Visitors may also see a film written and produced by Karl Keldermans that explains how a carillon is made and operates, a subject fascinating to adults and children alike.

Call 217-753-6219 for more information about this free festival.

Springfield, the state capital, offers many lodging options. Two downtown hotels are the Hilton and the Renaissance. Chain motels—including a Holiday Inn/Holidome Recreation Center, a Days Inn, and a Hampton Inn—can be found near the off-ramps of I-55, I-72, and I-36.

Springfield and central Illinois also have major historic sites relating to Abraham Lincoln. Young Abe grew to manhood on a farm in New Salem that is now a state park. The Lincoln Home National Historic Site (located in downtown Springfield at Eighth and Jackson Streets) is the only residence the family ever owned. As a young attorney, Lincoln had a law office on the corner of Sixth and Adams in a vintage building now partially restored. At Tenth and Monroe Streets, now the site of the Lincoln Depot Museum, the newly elected President Lincoln gave an eloquent speech before boarding the train to Washington, D.C., for the inauguration.

For more information about the Springfield area, call 800-545-7300.

Zionsville Country Market
Zionsville, Indiana

While many people claim that bigger is better, there's a community northwest of Indianapolis where people have shown that the reverse may be true. Here residents with a slow-growth policy have held on to what's best about small-town life: pleasing architecture where businesses and homes convey a turn-of-the-century feeling; well-tended lawns where friendly neighbors talk across the hedge; and an old-fashioned brick-paved Main Street where people can walk to buy sundries or clothing or gifts from shopkeepers they know.

Held each May on the first Saturday after Mother's Day, the Zionsville Country Market features a hundred and fifty art, crafts, and antique dealers from around the region who sell from booths along the village's Main Street. These exhibitors have been carefully screened to blend in with the more than fifty antique shops, art galleries, and boutiques that front the sidewalks behind them. As you browse from one booth to the next in Zionsville's downtown, you'll find pleasant dealers enjoying the shade of the festival's classy white tents.

Special attractions for children include clowns, jugglers, face painting, and free balloons that will grow as big as the youngsters' smiles. Food courts that serve everything from bratwurst to strawberries and ice cream make it possible to picnic on Main Street. Non-profit organizations use the income from food sales to carry on good works. If you need a Jump Start, there's a coffee shop by that name at 190 South Main Street. You'll also find a variety of restaurants in the area where the festival is held.

Souvenirs can be found everywhere, but why settle for an ordinary T-shirt? The setting for Country Market is a remarkable concentration of shops like Lilly's Boutique (209 South Main), Stacy LaBolts (125 West Sycamore), Harold's Haberdashery (140 South Main), and even The Children's Clothier (65 South Main). Clothing from Zionsville shops would make the most memorable souvenirs.

Horse carriage rides are available, but the most common way of getting around Zionsville is on foot. Festival-goers can park in one of two community lots and use complimentary shuttle transportation to reach the Country Market. Admission to the festival is free. **Contact the Zionsville Chamber of Commerce at 317-873-3836 for more information.**

Brick Street Inn Bed and Breakfast (317-873-9177) is a good place to try for accommodations. Some Zionsville residents claim that Monument Circle in the center of Indianapolis is only twenty minutes away, so northwest Indianapolis lodging might be another possibility. Embassy Suites North, Holiday Inn North, and Signature Inn North are well-located for this event.

Adam's Rib and Seafood House (40 South Main) is a long-running operation that features regional American dishes (317-873-3301). Z'Bistro (160 South Main) offers country French cuisine and is also well regarded (317-873-1888). Profitt's (65 South First Street) has homemade sandwiches, soups, and desserts.

Two other attractions in Zionsville are worthy of note. The Patrick Henry Sullivan Museum was made possible by a bequest from the great-granddaughter of the area's first settler. The brick building houses extensive genealogical records, and various community treasures. Zionsville's Lincoln Park, with its picturesque gazebo, was named for the president-elect who once gave a speech there when traveling by train to his inauguration in Washington.

Contact the Zionsville Chamber of Commerce (317-873-3836) for more information and phone numbers.

World Championship Old-Time Piano Playing Contest

Decatur, Illinois

Lots of people remember the first contest, held in 1975 in a warm and sunny outdoor spot near the Monticello Railway Museum where sponsors set up a piano. Contestants for the world championship pounded those ivories until winds and tornado warnings drove the players and some forty spectators to sheek shelter in an old baggage car. The contest winner turned out to be a seventy-one-year-old grandmother named Joybelle Squibb, and she stayed in that railroad car playing the crowd's favorite tunes as long as anyone would listen.

More than twenty years later, the World Championship Old-Time Piano Playing Contest usually takes place each year on Memorial Day Weekend at the Holiday Inn Conference Hotel in Decatur, Illinois. Over the years a spectator's orchestra, crowd sing-along, piano workshops, dealers' room, and musical parties have been been added to the championship competition. Contestants play in the traditional jazz, ragtime, and early stride styles once heard in bars and contests between 1890 and 1929.

Activities begin on Friday afternoon and end on Monday morning. The hour-long workshop sessions led by experts are open to players and non-players alike, and everyone who wants to gets to play. During first night parties, piano players gather in one room, and people who have brought other instruments gather in another, and everybody makes music.

The contest starts on Saturday morning with preliminary eliminations for regular- and junior-division piano players. Each player comes prepared to play a total of six selections (no medleys allowed). There's a break for lunch (somebody plays ragtime during the break); the program often continues until dinner.

The World's Greatest Sing-Along Show on Saturday night gives spectators a chance to sing more than fifty old melodies. Performers playing in various old-time styles take turns at the piano. In addition, the Old-Time Orchestra—which was supposed to have studied sheet music and practiced a bit on Friday evening—performs tunes like "Wedding Bells are

Breaking Up that Old Gang of Mine," making Saturday night a high time for all.

By Sunday afternoon the field has been narrowed to the ten or fewer players lucky enough to reach the semi-finals. The judges of past competitions have held impressive credentials: a professional musician and piano teacher, a university head of music theater, a ragtime piano player from New York, and a high-school music teacher. The junior champion usually plays during judging breaks so the place will stay filled with music.

Special food events round out the program. On Saturday evening "Dinner With the Champion" allows evening guests to meet with the previous year's champion. Past winners include Bruce Petsche, a steel company owner who also plays banjo; Janet Kaizer, a college teacher from Peoria; and Marty Mincer, a Hamburg, Iowa, apple grower whose grandmother started him on piano when he was eight years old.

Anyone interested in competing can write to the festival sponsors—the Old-Time Music Preservation Association—at Box 4714, Decatur, IL 62525. They'll send you the rules and an entry blank; return the form with the $20 entry fee, and they'll send you several free tickets.

Spectators may choose from various package options. A full weekend package includes accommodations for three nights; a ticket that allows entry to all events; personalized badges, a souvenir T-shirt, and a garter; the Saturday evening dinner (bring your own costume, if desired); the Sunday morning Coffee, Tea, and Memories gathering; and the Monday-morning brunch. Other options are also available; contact the Holiday Inn Conference Hotel at 217-422-8800 for more details.

Decatur itself has several museums and a number of good places to get outdoors and hike around. Architecture buffs may want to visit Milliken Place, a remarkable prairie-style development laid out in 1909, featuring houses and landscaping done by Walter Burley Griffin, Marion Mahony, and Frank Lloyd Wright. These three private homes are located at 1, 2, and 3 Milliken Place, and the entrance to the neighborhood is next to 125 Pine Street.

Call Decatur Area Convention and Visitor Information (800-252-3376 or 217-423-7000).

Heritage Preservation Fair
Greencastle, Indiana

The good folks of Greencastle, Indiana, celebrate National Heritage Preservation Week with a fair of their own held on the square in downtown Greencastle during the weekend after Mother's Day. Special activities include a Civil War Encampment, storytelling, a fiddler's contest, tours of historic buildings, demonstrations, street dancing, and even horse and carriage rides.

According to project director Tami Parker, adults especially enjoy the Civil War Ball, line dancing, historic exhibits, and carriage rides, while children have a street of their own with old-fashioned games, a balloon contest, face painting, and music.

Food booths sell tasty hamburger and sausage dishes; those in the know make their way toward Pap's Fillin' Station.

Admission is free, and four to five thousand people usually attend. **Call Tami Parker at 317-653-4927 for further information.**

Greencastle's Walden Inn, located on the campus of DePauw University, has fifty-five rooms and some Amish decorations. The well-regarded inn restaurant, A Different Drummer, is open to the public.

West of Greencastle in Putnam County, you can tour Parke County's covered bridges. Call the Convention and Visitors Bureau (317 569-5226) for information about lodging, dining, and attractions.

Norwegian dancers at the South Bend Ethnic Festival.

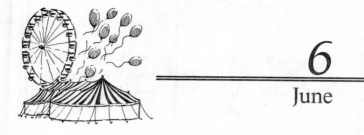

Indiana Lincoln Festival
Lincoln Boyhood National Memorial, Indiana

Along with Kentucky, where Lincoln was born, and Illinois, where he lived and practiced law before becoming president, Indiana also has a valid claim to the historic legacy of Abraham Lincoln. Young Abe spent his formative years in southern Indiana, where he attended a one-room school, worked on the family farm, and hauled grain to be ground at a nearby gristmill.

The Indiana Lincoln Festival, held at the Lincoln Boyhood National Memorial Visitors Center and Lincoln Living Historical Farm on a three-day weekend in mid-June, celebrates the fourteen years Abe Lincoln spent in the Hoosier state. During this weekend, the musical outdoor drama called Young Abe Lincoln opens the season at the Lincoln State Park nearby. Sponsored by the Lincoln Boyhood National Memorial, the show centers around the circumstances of Lincoln's youth and the pioneer lifestyle of the day.

The two-hundred-acre boyhood memorial encompasses a replica of Lincoln's boyhood home, a visitors center with a museum and interpretive displays, and a reconstructed farm of log buildings on the southwest corner of the original Lincoln homestead. Lincoln State Park contains the grave of Lincoln's only sister, the site of the early gristmill, and the 1,514-seat amphitheater in which the outdoor drama takes place. The restored brick home of Colonel William Jones was the residence of friends where Lincoln stayed when he returned to the area.

The Indiana Lincoln Festival takes place at all the above sites, as well as at the Holiday World Theme Park in the same area. Special theme films provide background information on Lincoln and his role in American history. Guided historical walks and educational talks about the nineteenth century also broaden the picture. Now and then an actor dressed as Abraham Lincoln strolls by. There are living-history demonstrations at the Lincoln boyhood farm. Craftspeople display and sell their wares, which are similar to the crafts settlers fashioned and used in pioneer times.

At Lincoln State Park there is a ladies' style show with models wearing clothing from the Civil War era. Uniformed soldiers take part in a Civil War encampment. Performances of Young Abe Lincoln are combined with a festive rail-splitter supper, consisting of hearty, traditional fare. There's also a snack bar at the state park, but little else; however, both parks are great places for picnics, so bring a full hamper and soft drinks for everyone.

South of Gentryville, follow the signs to the Jones House State Historic Site, where there's a Lincoln look-alike contest—now, that's living history! You can also take a candlelight tour of the home that was once the centerpiece of a log-cabin community called Jonesboro.

An admission fee is charged at the Lincoln Boyhood National Memorial and also at Lincoln State

Park. About three thousand people usually attend the festival, which can be reached via I-64, exiting south onto US 231, then turning east on State 162. The signs that say "Lincoln Parks" are helpful, but the Lincoln City road is a wrong turn! The entrances to the national memorial and the state park are almost across the road from each other. **For more information about the Indiana Lincoln Festival call 812-937-4541.**

Nearby places to stay include the towns of Dale, Huntingburg, Jasper, Rockport, and Tell City, all within a twenty-four-mile radius. There are chain motels (Holiday Inn, Days Inn, Best Western) and independent lodgings; RV campgrounds are located in Lincoln State Park, near Tell City, and at Patoka Lake.

South Bend Ethnic Festival
South Bend, Indiana

In 1974, local movers and shakers launched the South Bend Ethnic Festival as a lead-in to the 1976 Bicentennial Year. Their aim was to celebrate the rich ethnic heritage of the local community. That first year, St. Andrew's Greek Orthodox Church ran a Greek booth, the First Unitarian Church operated a lemonade stand, and St. Stephen's church had a Mexican booth; they've done the same thing each year as the event has grown. The South Bend Ethnic Festival draws enthusiastic visitors from more than twenty states for a family-oriented weekend supported by many dedicated individuals and corporations in the area.

Held in early summer each year in downtown South Bend near the St. Joseph River, the three-day event features over one hundred and fifty food and crafts booths; lively entertainment on four different outdoor stages; and a parade with nearly one hundred bands, floats, and marching groups. Laugh at the clowns, salute the policemen, marvel at the beauty queens—this parade has it all. The great stream of participants moves along Jefferson Boulevard from downtown across the bridge and through Howard Park. During past years, there have been lovely blossom-time floats, rollerblade skaters, and even a float carrying the Redding family reunion!

During the festival, three blocks of Michigan Street become the festival midway. The booths with their bright awnings and umbrella shades turn the thoroughfare into a festive gathering place, for they line both sides of the street between Washington and Western Avenue.

A copy of the annual tabloid program and festival guide, published by the *Penny Saver/Times,* has a two-page map inside that shows the location and specialty of each booth. Take note of the additional booths in off-street locations, or you'll miss exhibits like Renata Kelly's Handmade Sweaters, crafts from thirty developing countries, and the dunk tank, where local radio personalities raise money for charity by getting soaked.

Overall, there's a vast range of items for sale: needlepoint, African jewelry, balloons, silver jewelry, silk flowers, crafts from Guatemala, and ceramics from Peru. It's a trip around the world without leaving South Bend. A three-block stroll down Michigan Street can also be a world-wide tasting session. Elephant Ears—usually paired with lemonade and sold in several places—have become a popular Hoosier festival treat. The distinctive shape comes from stretching and shaping the dough balls before frying them. Here's a recipe:

Heat together, but do not boil
    1½ cups milk
    2 tablespoons sugar
    1 teaspoon salt
    6 tablespoons shortening
until shortening is melted. Cool to lukewarm. Add
    2 packets dry yeast
    4 cups flour
by putting in the flour 2 cups at a time and beating until smooth after each addition. Put the dough in a greased bowl, cover with a damp cloth, and let rise until doubled in size (maybe 30 minutes). Pour cooking oil into a large, heavy skillet or pot until oil is over an inch deep. Heat oil to 350° F. Dust your hands with flour and pinch off golf-ball-sized dough balls. Stretch each one into a thin 6- to 8-inch circle. Drop each "ear" of stretched dough into the hot oil and fry until it rises to the surface. Then turn it and fry the other side until light brown. Drain on absorbent paper and sprinkle with a mixture of
    1/2 cup sugar
    1 teaspoon cinnamon.

That's just one treat. You can also expect to encounter Vietnamese spring rolls, Dutch soft pretzels, Hungarian cabbage, Jamaican curried goat, West Indian fruit, Cajun wings, Greek baklava, Hawaiian shaved ice (shaved ice covered with flavored drink in a glass). Of course, since this is the Midwest there'll be hamburgers, hot dogs, soft drinks, popcorn, and ice cream.

Each of the outdoor stages offers ethnic entertainment at intervals throughout the festival day.
Whether it's story tellers, blues groups, Irish
folksingers, Hispanic dancers, bagpipes, polkas, or
Native American drums, something will surely set your
feet tapping. The grand finale, held in Howard Park, is
a free community concert under the stars.

The South Bend Ethnic Festival has something
of interest to nearly everyone. Parents who want a
break for a while can take their kids across the river
to the children's area in Howard Park. Sponsored by
the YMCA, the children's area offers kid-pleasing
amusements, such as rides in little airplanes, go-carts,
and trains. Families can also take part in a teddy-bear
toss and a basketball competition complete with prizes
for all.

Those shirts, pins, hats, and plastic cups found
at the Ethnic Festival all have such distinctive designs
because the Pitcock Design Group supports the event
by donating their services to design these items. The
festival motif usually involves food. One year there
was a Polynesian food god; another year it was a South
Sea Island duo carrying baskets filled with fresh food.
South Bend residents who attend each year display collections of these items in shops and homes.

The City of South Bend holds the Ethnic Festival
on the Fourth of July weekend (or sometimes the
weekend after) every year in downtown South Bend.
An estimated one hundred thousand people attend the
festival over a three-day period. **Call 800-780-2349 for
more information.**

The South Bend Marriott stands quite close to the center of festival action. When you call to reserve a room, ask about their special summer event rates. Two other possibilities are the Holiday Inn Downtown and the Morris Inn (on the Notre Dame campus north of the city). South Bend also has charming bed and breakfasts, including the Book Inn (five rooms in an elegantly furnished French Victorian home), and the Queen Anne Inn (another elegant Victorian home with Frank Lloyd Wright bookcases and original wall fabrics). Both are located near the festival in a central historic area on West Washington Street.

In addition to the array of ethnic foods sold from festival booths, downtown South Bend has many fine restaurants. The Lasalle Grill serves dinner in a smart, bistro-like setting at 115 West Colfax; call for reservations. Also downtown, the Marriott Hotel (123 North St. Joseph Street) has tables in a glassed-in atrium. Tippecanoe Place (620 West Washington Street) offers steaks and seafood in the renovated 1888 Studebaker mansion.

During the festival, you'll probably walk right by the Century Center. Inside, there's a theater and convention hall, along with a museum that depicts the development of the Studebaker automobiles once manufactured in South Bend. There's also a great view of the St. Joseph River through a window a hundred and thirty feet long and thirty-eight feet high.

The Studebaker National Museum (524 South Main Street) contains vehicles from 1852 through 1966, plus a science and technology center and a gift shop. The new College Football Hall of Fame is located downtown on Washington Street across from the Marriott.

If you'd like to spend some time outside, South Bend has developed a series of parks (Leeper, Pinhook Rum Village, and others) bordering the St. Joseph River and connected by a river walk. In yet another park southeast of downtown (via Jefferson Avenue and Greenlawn), the zoo at Potawatomi Park has animals from five continents.

The University of Notre Dame involves much more than the famous Fighting Irish. This educational enterprise actually began in the nineteenth century, when a priest named Edward Sorin founded a mission school for Potawatomi Indians on a site now part of the campus. If you see nothing else, drive by the university's famous golden dome atop the administration building. The figure crowning the dome represents the Virgin Mary.

For more information about lodging, dining, and attractions in the area, call 219-234-0051 or 800-392-0051.

Festival of the Fish
Vermilion, Ohio

Fishing has long been a means of survival on the shores of Lake Erie; first the Native Americans fished from their bark canoes, and then the Voyageurs and the pioneers followed their example. On a good day—and there have been many of them—the men who went down to the lake to fish came home with a creel full of food for the family. Walleye, yellow perch, smallmouth bass, and other varieties can still be caught near the Lake Erie shore, and riding the waves in a boat is as much fun as ever.

The Festival of the Fish, held each Father's Day weekend in Vermilion, Ohio, celebrates this fishing tradition, as well as the lovely early days of the summer season. Located in northwestern Ohio where the Vermilion River flows into Lake Erie, the community holds this event at scattered locations near the water.

The three-day celebration begins at noon on Friday, when the midway opens. The town usually imports high-quality carnival rides from Cleveland and sets them up near the sponsoring organization, St. Mary's Church on Exchange Street. After the pet parade, usually held in front of the Main Street stage, owners take home huge trophies for the best pet trick, most unusual pet, and for the pet and owner dressed in the best nautical costumes.

Princess pageants and a fashion show follow, promising something for all. The Best Father and Best Grandfather come forward, the winners chosen in an essay contest for schoolchildren.

Evening brings the crowning of the new queen. As a Vermilion ambassador, she will spend time during the following year visiting people in hospitals around the region. A band plays classic Motown hits, and those who aren't dancing usually get nostalgic about the '50s and '60s.

The YMCA hosts a number of family activities: a volleyball tournament, foot races for ages four to adult, even a one-mile competition for seniors. Face painting, a home-run derby, field-goal kicking, a foot-ball toss, and free-throw shooting contests offer variety. Science activities organized by a children's museum involve water rockets, a catapult that throws water grenades, giant bubble wands, zoom balls, and turtle races. There are surely science lessons there somewhere, but it sounds more like flat-out fun!

The Crazy Craft race begins at noon at the foot of South Street, where you can watch from the bank. Creativity reigns as people drift by on anything that floats. Rock bands and a talented magician provide a choice of entertainment in different places. After that, the local firemen who used to sponsor a water fight now hold a chicken barbecue.

Afterwards you can wander down to the waterfront to watch the starlight boat parade, which begins at dusk. Boats cruise down the Vermilion from the public dock and putt-putt around the lagoons, competing for cash prizes. Sparkling lights on the water, music in the air, and lovely reflections come in the wake of a very full day.

Sunday brings a land parade, with the Father and Grandfather winners featured as local heroes. There are also bands, community and business floats, policemen, and firemen involved—everyone supports the Festival of the Fish.

Festival attendance usually reaches forty thousand to fifty thousand and there is no admission charge. **Contact the Vermilion Chamber of Commerce at 216-967-4477 for more information.**

Lancaster Old Car Club Spring Festival
Lancaster, Ohio

Back in 1957, Edson Devore and some neighbors in a small town southeast of Columbus, Ohio, organized the Lancaster Old Car Club. Their first annual festival and swap meet grew over three decades to become an annual event in which five hundred of the Midwest's best cars compete in forty different categories for a hundred and twenty trophies.

The Lancaster Old Car Club Spring Festival takes place during the first weekend in June. Held at the Fairfield County Fairgrounds in Lancaster, Ohio (about thirty miles southeast of Columbus via US 33), the gathering draws old-car aficionados from Ohio, Indiana, Michigan, Pennsylvania, West Virginia, Kentucky, and even more distant places.

During the Swap Meet held on both days, two hundred and fifty vendors sell antique auto parts and related items from reserved spaces on the grounds. Visitors can wander through this flea market of car parts to shop for an old carburetor or running board while browsing and visiting with friends.

The cars in the Sunday competition are not for sale, but much selling takes place during the Saturday morning auction, at which sellers (it is claimed) may well get higher prices than expected, and buyers (it is also claimed) may even go home convinced they've just bought bargains—thus, everyone wins. Another trading opportunity is the Car Corral. On Sunday, several dozen car sellers (who pay fees) display their vehicles in a special area.

On Saturday afternoon there's a "Cruise" event—a gathering of people with older cars (from the fifties, sixties, and seventies) that don't happen to be in the competition. Radios blare fifties crooners and rock classics, and those who date back far enough talk about the fun they had in high school. Back then, a crucial part of one's education was cruising around the drive-ins on Saturday night.

On both days of the festival, the Hocking Valley Steam and Antique Power Club displays several dozen old work machines. Visitors can see old steam- and gasoline-powered engines, tractors, thrashers, sawmills, corn shredders, and the like—many of them still up and running. This open-air museum of working equipment spans several decades of agricultural and industrial history. Asserts one regular attendee, "The steam show is always a hit."

The climax of the festival is the presentation of trophies on Sunday. Participants in the competitions must register their cars (original unrestored, modified, or restored to original specifications) by 11:00 A.M. Sunday to be eligible to compete. Each entrant pays a fee and gets a reserve parking place and a plaque. About five hundred cars are entered in categories that include Ford T, Model A, classic (1930-1948), fire truck (through 1969), motorcycle (through 1969), Corvette (through 1971), foreign car, muscle car, street rod, and others from 1896 through 1979.

The older set—especially those who are over sixty—will appreciate the Antique Filling Station Museum. This vintage 1930 structure on the grounds is filled with car-care memorabilia. Curators encourage people to donate anything appropriate, so bring whatever you have.

Make sure the kids get inside the track to walk through the Steam Show while the antique power engines are in action. This kind of thing may not sound too cool when you describe it, but their enthusiasm could well surprise them.

The Lancaster Old Car Club and The Hocking Valley Steam and Antique Car Club are the only food and drink vendors on the grounds. Because they have to feed thousands of people "quick calories" over a two-day period, they offer sandwiches, ice cream, bratwurst, and pies. If your tastes run more to whole grains, fresh fruits, and vegetables, just bring that healthy stuff along.

The best place to browse for car-related souvenirs is the Swap Meet, unless, of course, you're looking for a sleek T-bird convertible from a vintage year—quite a souvenir.

Admission is free, but expect a parking fee. There's no charge for walking in, wandering around, and looking, but there are fees for participating in awards competitions, for selling at the Swap Meet, for entering the Cruise, and for selling at the Car Corral. Attendance is usually around twenty thousand. The entrance to the fairgrounds is at North Broad Street and Fair Avenue in the north part of Lancaster.

Lancaster has several motels near the exits on US 33 (also called Memorial Drive) and some downtown, as well as east on Main Street. **For more information call the Fairfield County Visitors and Convention**

Bureau (800-626-1296). For lodging in Columbus (half an hour away), call the Greater Columbus Convention and Visitors Bureau (614-221-6623 or 800-345-4FUN).

Shaw's Restaurant, 123 North Broad Street, Lancaster, has a seasonal menu and cocktail lounge. Mauger's Seafood at 512 East Main Street serves lunches and dinners with beer and wine.

Other attractions in Lancaster include charmingly restored early-nineteenth-century homes within a square bounded by Main, Broad, High, and Wheeling Streets. The Sherman House Museum (137 East Main Street) honors the famous Civil War general and his brother, author of the Sherman Anti-Trust Act.

For a change of pace, visit Mount Pleasant in nearby Rising Park. This flat-topped sandstone rock formation was used as a lookout by Native Americans and early settlers. Six miles south of Lancaster via US 33, Wahkeenah Nature Preserve has a museum and nature trails. Rhododendron, ferns, native orchids, and white-tailed deer can be seen on this wooded site.

Grant Park Music Festival
Chicago, Illinois

A long-time Chicago resident and avid festival-goer chooses her words carefully, because describing the scene is not the same as experiencing it, she believes. "There's great music by interesting composers outdoors, right on the lakefront," Judy Brown explains. "It's a free concert and also a great people-watching adventure. On a summer evening, the weather's great.

There's music coming from the band shell, a beautiful view of the skyline, and sailboats out on the lake."

The Grant Park Music Festival, sponsored by the Chicago Park District, is a series of performances held each summer between June and August. The festival consists of nearly three dozen outdoor, night-time concerts held in Grant Park throughout the season. The Concerts for Kids series is a related series of ten classical music performances scheduled during mornings and evenings. The Grant Park Concerts Society, formed in 1977, helps maintain the quality of both events and ensures their public accessibility.

"No other city offers a full-scale series of free outdoor symphony concerts at so high an artistic level," claimed a Chicago music critic before the 1994 season opened.

Judy Brown and countless others have been attending Grant Park symphony concerts since the 1950s, when a "sea of admirers" came to hear Van Cliburn. At the Grant Park concert there's a reserved (paid) section close to the band shell, she explains; the best open (free) seats are benches behind them. The orchestra may be playing the music of Leroy Anderson or Dvorák or Strauss while people picnic on the lawn beneath the trees.

"You can walk in off the street and hear a symphony under the stars," Brown claims, including "sophisticated musical artists on their way up."

When pianist Van Cliburn opened the Grant Park Music Festival concert series in 1994, he played before an audience of three hundred and fifty thousand. The following year, soprano Frederica von Stade launched the 1995 series before similar crowds. Music may range from the Fanfare John Williams wrote for the 1984 Olympic Games to a symphonic rendition of a Hungarian gypsy dance arranged by Brahms.

Adults could organize a city escape weekend around a combination of Chicago lakefront hotel accommodations, relaxed restaurant lunches, and the Grant Park concerts. The park runs along Chicago's famous Michigan Avenue shopping corridor, and the Petrillo Music Shell is within walking distance of major hotels and restaurants.

Bringing the kids works too, because nobody minds their presence. In fact, just about everyone comes, from month-old babes in arms to wrinkled great-grandmothers.

There is no admission charge, but a small donation will reserve you a seat. The proceeds from donations go to advertise the festival and pay the fees for solo artists and guest conductors. About two million people attend some part of the series during the season. **Call the Grant Park Concerts Society (312-819-0614) for more information.**

Nearby hotels include the Hyatt Regency Chicago, the Palmer House Hilton, Holiday Inn, and Days Inn on Lakeshore Drive. An airport shuttle provides transportation between downtown hotels and O'Hare International Airport. Call the Chicago Office of Tourism (312-744-2400 or 800-487-2446) for details.

Indiana Black Expo Summer Celebration
Indianapolis, Indiana

In 1971, a group of religious and civic leaders in Indianapolis organized an exposition that would showcase the achievements of African-Americans in different fields such as art, history, and economics. The volunteers worked hard; the people who came to that first festival learned a lot, and also had a good time! Since that first expo held at the fairgrounds, the Indiana Black Expo (IBE) Summer Celebration has grown into the largest event of its kind. Visitors learn about education, business development, political action, the arts, health and fitness programs, religion, and sports, and listen to top-flight entertainers. What's more, the IBE has become a not-for-profit community service agency found in key areas throughout the state.

The Indiana Black Expo Summer Celebration, a major festival held at the Indiana Convention Center and RCA Dome south of Monument Circle and at other sites around Indianapolis, involves more than a thousand exhibits, along with activities for various age groups, ecumenical church services, competitions, parties, employment opportunities, performances, luncheons, awards programs, receptions, sporting events, family reunions, and conference sessions on major family and neighborhood issues. Held in summer, the festival runs for a week on a daily schedule that starts with early-morning breakfast meetings and winds down during late-night music sessions.

The Indiana Black Expo celebrated its twenty-fifth anniversary in 1995. They now operate from their headquarters on North Meridian Street in Indianapolis with a board of thirty-five members, a full-time staff of eighteen, hundreds of enthusiastic volunteers, and the support of more than a dozen major corporations.

As it was in the beginning, the goal of the IBE is still to create and maintain an awareness of African-American culture and heritage. But they don't just sit back and talk about it. They're heavily involved in youth programs, employment and business development, and myriad other activities directed at individuals and society. They also award $50,000 in scholarships each year.

Then there's the festival itself. At the Summer Celebration all sorts of events go on before the official grand opening. On Sunday, there may be special church services held throughout the city.

Children may be very glad they've come when they learn about Soulfest, a three-day event that kicks off the Summer Celebration. Soulfest features carnival rides, a slam-dunk basketball contest for young people, basketball and softball tournaments, entertainment, exhibits, vendors, and ethnic foods.

There are many fairs within this festival: an employment opportunity fair, a health fair, and an art exhibition and reception for the grand opening. The governor's and president's receptions are usually by invitation only. Parties after big events include appearances by Expo celebrities. Bill Cosby, the Reverend Jesse Jackson, Dionne Warwick, Spike Lee, and Rosa Parks are some who have appeared in past years. A music-heritage festival held during one Summer Celebration drew Keith Washington, Rachelle Farrell, Out Kast, Usher, and A Few Good Men as performers.

Later that night, adult entertainment involved jazz, reggae, and rhythm and blues in different locations within The Culture Club.

Flip the pages of an annual program and there's certainly lots to choose from: Jesse Jackson speaking on Operation Breadbasket; the Hair Wars, a beauty fair and styling competition; a Youth Summit program on problems and solutions; a boxing tournament; the "We Can Feed the Hungry" program; a fashion show; more entertainment at the Indiana University track and field stadium; a party starring the comedian Just June; a Kid's World program; finals in the gospel-singing competition; a third night of entertainment with big name performers; a conference on family and neighborhood issues such as education, rebuilding neighborhoods, combating drugs, and solving the crisis of violence.

Admission is charged for most events, although some are free. **Call 317-925-2702 for more information.**

One of the festival packages available includes two nights' lodging. Another includes meals, but no hotel. The program lists some eighteen hotels and motels in the city of Indianapolis.

Festival-goers may eat from food booths or take part in special breakfasts and dinners. The large, indoor City Market, located north of the convention center at 222 East Market Street, sells meats, cheeses, baked goods, fresh fruit, and assorted ethnic foods in a renovated 1886 market building. On fine days, locals buy picnic foods here and enjoy them on the Monument Circle Plaza.

A nearby attraction is the Madame Walker Urban Life Center and Theatre at 617 Indiana Avenue. Housed in the renovated Walker Theater, it was built in 1927 to honor Madame C. J. Walker, a black woman who became the first self-made woman millionaire in America. Various cultural events take place here and visitors may take tours of the building. Call 317-236-2099 for information; call 317-236-2087 for tickets.

Strawberry Festival
Indianapolis, Indiana

"Strawberry Festival" and "sponsored by a church" could well mean a gathering in a country churchyard at some tiny Hoosier crossroads. Guess again. This big event takes place in downtown Indianapolis around Monument Circle, where thousands of people gather to feast on homemade shortcakes piled high with ice cream, sweet berries, and whipped cream. The proceeds go to support charitable causes near and far. **Call Christ Church Cathedral (317-636-4577).**

Vevay Horse Pull
Vevay, Indiana

Indiana farmers hold a Horse Pull, the largest in the southern part of the state, at the Switzerland County 4-H fairgrounds on a Saturday in mid-June. Draft horses and their owners compete for trophies and over $2,000 in prize money. Teams come from all around the Midwest. There's no charge to enter and no charge to watch. Lodging can be found in Vevay. **Call 812-427-2670 for more information.**

Indiana Fiddlers Gathering
Battle Ground, Indiana

N ear the end of June, people who love traditional folk and country music gather in Tippecanoe Battlefield Memorial Park in Battle Ground for a three-day festival at which talented musicians play fiddles, banjos, dulcimers, harps, and string bass. The typical program goes beyond traditional American borders to include Eastern European and even Paraguayan music. A special children's concert, music workshops, and dancing (contra and square) add to the fun.

Quilt-makers and regional artists also display their work. The Tippecanoe Battlefield Museum (at the site) is usually open for visitors to see displays and browse in the gift shop. During the festival, refreshments can be bought on the grounds, or you can investigate Battle Ground's one restaurant. Many visitors bring well-stocked coolers, picnic blankets, and lawn chairs. **Call 317-742-1419 for more information.**

Railroad Days
Galesburg, Illinois

T he community of Galesburg owes much to the railroads and salutes them each year with the Railroad Days Festival. Held during the fourth weekend in June, the event features a carnival, a flea market, a parade, a concert, model-railroad displays, a block

Fiddlers tune up for three days of old-time music in Battle Ground, Indiana.

party, a fun run, a showcase of cars, displays of railroad equipment, a basketball contest, a bake sale, a craft show, and train excursion rides.

Colton Park Railroad Museum has a collection of rolling stock and railroad memorabilia housed in an old Pullman car. Retired railroaders can usually be found waiting eagerly for a chance to explain things to visitors.

The poet Carl Sandburg was born and buried in Galesburg. The town has Amtrak service, so consider coming to Galesburg by train. The town boasts nearly a dozen motels and small inns. **Call the Galesburg Convention and Visitors Bureau, 319-343-1194, for more information.**

Chautauqua means speakers, theater, musicians, and weeks of family fun.

Fountain Park Chautauqua
Remington, Indiana

Halfway between Chicago and Indianapolis, in a wooded setting near the town of Remington, a few hundred people gather for two weeks every year for what may be the country's oldest chautauqua. Within a circle of cottages, there's a small hotel and an open-air tabernacle. While children dart here and there across the grassy lawn, their elders socialize on the cottage walks, play checkers on a screened-in porch, or sneak a catnap on a squeaky bunk bed.

Fountain Park Chautauqua begins in late July and runs through the first two weeks of August. Held at Fountain Park (one mile north of Remington and a half mile west of US 231) the chautauqua offers wholesome recreation for the family, including entertaining daily and evening programs, an art colony and classes, and a quilt show and classes. Here, several generations spend a few hours or two weeks together, renewing their ties to family, friends, and country.

The early chautauquas, many of them held under tents, were the adult- education programs of their day. This "education under canvas" was highly valued by women, because social pressure, heavy work, and a large number of children often kept them close to home.

The modern programs at Fountain Park run the gamut from herbalist to barbershop singers to a troupe of young kids doing vaudeville routines. Each Sunday morning there are Christian services in the renovated tabernacle. The Women's Improvement Association meets each Wednesday afternoon—apparently they have given up on trying to improve the men!

Here and there around the park, artists with paint tubes and easels register impressions of the old fountain, the rambling wood frame hotel, or the round face of a child. Classes for adults and for young people meet daily. Patrons of the arts and prospective patrons gather each year for a special tea.

The Fountain Park Chautauqua—known as Park to regular attendees—celebrated its one-hundredth anniversary during the summer of 1995. Some say only one other chautauqua in the country has as long a history as this one.

The original plan for this lovely wooded land along Carpenter Creek involved an outdoor assembly where people could gather to discuss religious, scientific, and literary subjects. Over time, its uses varied as the property changed owners. The first ten-day session in 1895 centered around church services given by a popular revivalist. Visitors took lodging in rented tents. By the second season, the assembly offered a full, rounded program, and people paid $1.00 admission for the ten-day event.

A thirty-six-room hotel was completed before the Fountain Park Chautauqua season began in 1898. A dam across the Creek formed a lagoon where visitors rode in paddleboats powered by small boys. Visitors arrived on horseback, by train, by hack, or in their own horse-drawn buggies. By 1901, cottages stood here and there at the edge of the property. The program featured a member of Congress, an inspiring 102-year-old woman born in Ireland, a missionary on furlough from India, and a troupe of bell ringers.

By 1905, the assembly had become successful largely because of the high quality of its programs. As a visiting senator described the gathering, "Here was freedom; rest for the weary, religion, history, romance, right living, higher aims, education, music, good fellowship; everything except the sordid aim to accumulate money . . ."

Hazel Brown, Carl and Ray Culp, and others born early in the century still enjoy the same chautauqua they attended each year as kids. Hazel Brown recalls big-name speakers like Billy Sunday and William Jennings Bryan. The audience came from miles around to hear them, many traveling by horse and buggy.

"When William Jennings Bryan came to speak, I would have been nine or ten years old," Brown recalls. "My mother told me, 'I want you—instead of walking around the park—to go into the tabernacle and sit down and listen!'"

Fountain Park provides many opportunities for grown-ups to socialize, spend time on hobbies, and eat. The cottages and other buildings circle a wide, grassy lawn much as pioneer wagons once formed a protective enclosure around travelers camped for the night. With all the cars safely parked outside the cottage circle, children can enjoy the run of the place—

swinging on playground equipment, bowling on the green, joining in group games—while their parents keep an eye on them.

Many chautauqua visitors stay for the full two weeks in one of the modest cottages or in RVs parked nearby. Others book motel rooms east of Remington (near I-65) and come and go from there. Guests at the thirty-three-room Fountain Park Hotel take their meals in the hundred-and-fifty-seat dining room (the rate includes three meals a day). Visitors may join the hotel guests for breakfast, lunch, or dinner if they make reservations. Behind the scenes, cooks prepare a set meal, served more or less at the stated time. The menu resembles a catered church supper, with filling, down-home farm fare such as chicken and noodles, pickled beets, green beans with ham, or maybe a taco salad. Quench your thirst with lemonade or iced tea.

Quilts or quilted wall hangings made by people who come to Fountain Park every year make memorable keepsakes. Browse among the artists' paintings. Someone may be making hand-crafted dolls. In the hotel lobby you'll find inexpensive mementos, like old postcards that show the early hotel and fountain for which the park is named.

Audrey Casey Watts, who managed the Fountain Park Hotel for years, was known for her friends, her quick humor, and her creative way with regional foods. She had a large repertoire of quick-mix and make-ahead dishes and specialized in recipes that looked hard but—according to her—were easy. This is her recipe (taken from the Culp Family Cookbook) for the Pizza Casserole served at the Fountain Park Hotel:

Pizza Casserole
1 pound ground beef
¼ teaspoon basil
1 large onion, chopped
1 14-ounce jar pizza sauce
1 green pepper, chopped
1 8-ounce package macaroni
½ teaspoon garlic salt
1 13½-ounce package sliced pepperoni
¼ teaspoon pepper
1 4-ounce package cheddar cheese
¼ teaspoon oregano
Cook beef, onions, and pepper in a large skillet; drain
well; put into a large pan. Add salt, pepper, oregano,
basil, and pizza sauce; stir well. Cover, reduce heat,
and simmer 15 minutes.
Boil macaroni without salt. Drain and add to meat and
mix well. Transfer to lightly greased 12 x 8 x 2 inch
pan. Top with pepperoni and cover with foil. Bake at
350 degrees for 20 minutes. Uncover and top with
cheese; bake uncovered for 5 more minutes. Serves 8.

Admission is charged. **For more information,
call Laurene Mykrantz at 219-261-2714, before Fountain Park. During the chautauqua, call 219-261-3220
(Fountain Park Hotel).**

For hotel information, call Dorothy Wilken
(manager) at 219-261-2747, before Fountain Park.
During Fountain Park, call 219-261-3220 (Fountain
Park Hotel).

For RV space, call Bill Yoder at 219-583-3978.

Football's Greatest Weekend

Canton, Ohio

For three days each summer thousands of fans from around the world gather in Canton, Ohio, for events that celebrate the sport of football. These events take place in downtown Canton at the Canton Civic Center, the Fawcett Stadium, and the Pro Football Hall of Fame.

Football aficionados who arrive on Thursday dressed in their casual best kick off the festival at the Ribs Burnoff, a barbecue rib cookout. Thus fortified, they meet, mingle, and relax a bit before watching the fireworks at the end of the day.

Men in suits and ties and women in day dresses move through Friday's festive events: the mayor's breakfast, a fashion show, and a civic dinner honoring this year's enshrinees. Jim Finks, Henry Jordan, Steve Largent, Lee Roy Selmon, and Kellen Winslow were enshrined in the Pro Football Hall of Fame in 1995.

The big festival parade takes place on Saturday morning in the streets of downtown Canton. The enshrinement ceremonies follow, held on the steps of the Pro Football Hall of Fame. There are about fifteen hundred public seats for visitors, and additional thousands crowd whatever standing room they can find. A special pro game follows (the Panthers and the Jaguars played in 1995) in the stadium across the street.

"Where the Season Never Ends" is a fitting slogan for the Pro Football Hall of Fame, which is open every day of the year but Christmas. Built in the town where the National Football League was founded in

1920, the museum is actually a four-building complex with exhibition areas, a movie theater, a research library, a snack bar, a museum store, and large twin enshrinement halls. The display for each person in the hall of fame includes a bronze bust and biographical information. Exhibits have been developed with bright graphics and dramatic action photos, and many of the displays are interactive. The museum shop carries mementos representing each of the National Football League's twenty-eight teams, as well as Pro Football Hall of Fame items.

You can order tickets for the pro game through the Pro Football Hall of Fame (216-456-8207). Note that many people return each year, and the few hundred tickets available for this game sell out early. Order tickets for other Football's Greatest Weekend events from the Greater Canton Chamber of Commerce (216-456-7253); you should ask them about lodging and dining. If the Canton motels are full, try Akron (thirty miles north) or New Philadelphia (thirty miles south). Canton and the Pro Football Hall of Fame are an hour south of Cleveland via I-77.

Festival of Flight
Wapakoneta, Ohio

Held each July near the anniversary of Neil Armstrong's historic walk on the moon, the Festival of Flight celebrates various achievements in flight and space exploration. There's a Spirit of America radio-controlled airplane show, a model-rocket launch, and a ham-radio demonstration. Food booths provide energy, and games offer entertainment for the whole family.

The Neil Armstrong Air and Space Museum pays thoughtful tribute to Armstrong and to others who have risked much to learn more about flight and space. The contemporary-style museum, with its striking white dome and roof rising up from a field, contrasts dramatically with the sleepy village of Wapakoneta, where many older residents remember Armstrong as a boy. Amble from one exhibit to the next to learn about the Wright Brothers and other early experimenters in flight; study the Gemini VIII earth orbiter and the intricate Apollo space suits; and experience simulated travel into space in the Astrotheater and the Infinity Room.

For more information about the Festival of Flight, call the Neil Armstrong Air and Space Museum (419-738-8811). Call the Lima–Allen County Convention and Visitors Bureau (419-222-6045) for information about lodging, dining, and other area attractions.

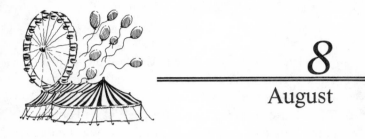

8

August

Coshocton Canal Festival
Coshocton, Ohio

Like other midwestern states, Ohio became involved in a grand canal-building scheme during the depression that followed the War of 1812. The plan called for a navigable waterway reaching all the way from Cleveland on Lake Erie to Marietta on the Ohio River—a distance of three hundred and eight miles. A town then called Port Roscoe, halfway between the two cities, welcomed the first canal boat in August 1831.

During the third weekend in August, the Coshocton Canal Festival celebrates the area's colorful history for three days near a section of the old canal. Roscoe Village, where some of the events take place, is a restored nineteenth-century canal town with early homes, shops, and a museum with exhibits depicting canal days.

On Saturday, a Grand Parade moves down Whitewoman Street, the main street through the town of Coshocton. Many floats represent modes of transportation from an earlier time, and most are pulled by draft horses. The Canal Queen and Princess ride by. There may be a Conestoga wagon. Flags wave. Bands march. Many participants wear typical period clothing from the canal era. There's even an early fire engine.

The Canal Days Arts and Crafts show—a juried event—features nineteenth-century crafts such as woven fabrics, tole painting on wood, and metalwork. Three judges selected by the Roscoe Village Foundation evaluate the craftspeople, so the show is limited to a hundred and thirty-five. Town officials close off a section of Whitewoman Street, where craftspeople exhibit in booths or under tents that provide shelter if there's a downturn in the weather.

Visitors to the festival can take part in many contests such as beard growing, hog calling, or pie baking. Local school children compete in an old-time spelling bee, and many prizes are awarded.

Canal boat rides on a restored segment of the early canal take place all season as well as during the festival. Passengers climb aboard a replica of an early canal boat and are pulled along the water by sturdy horses at the speed of two miles an hour. The canal boat, which holds a hundred and twenty people, operates daily between Memorial Day and Labor Day and on weekends through mid-October (admission charged).

The town of Coshocton was once the capital of the Delaware Indian territory, inhabited by east-coast tribal people who migrated westward.

The Coshocton Canal Festival, sponsored jointly by the Roscoe Village Foundation and the Coshocton County Chamber of Commerce, has much to interest all ages. The Johnson Humrickhouse Museum in Roscoe Village, for example, houses interesting Native American and Oriental artifacts. Children will enjoy the pet parade, a ride on a paddleboat, or swimming at

Coshocton Lake Park. Be sure to peek inside the restored buildings of Roscoe Village, where costumed interpreters describe the canal-era lifestyle.

During the festival, street vendors hawk peanuts, soft pretzels, popcorn, and lemonade. There are old-fashioned sandwiches, ice cream, and baked goods as well. The favorite festival food is fresh, roasted sweet corn dripping with butter.

When choosing a souvenir from the eighteenth-century items made by modern craftspeople, I usually look for something with a modern use, such as a pottery mug, a woven scarf, or a leather carryall.

For more information, call 800-338-4724 or 614-622-9310.

The Roscoe Village Inn (200 North Whitewoman Street) has a country-inn ambience. Ask about bicycle rental. Other motor inns and motels can be found in the Coshocton area. The Old Warehouse Restaurant (400 North Whitewoman Street) is a restored 1838 building with a canal-days atmosphere.

Nearby Dresden is the home of Longaberger Baskets. Visitors can tour the factory to see them made.

Brickyard 400 Festival
Indianapolis, Indiana

The Brickyard 400 is an annual stock-car race on the NASCAR circuit that takes place on the same track as the Indianapolis 500. The two-and-one-half-mile oval, paved with 3.2 million bricks early in the century, originated as a testing ground for the regional auto industry. The Brickyard was subsequently used for several racing contests. Though almost the entire track has been covered with asphalt, one token strip of the earlier brick surface remains.

In 1911, the track's owners decided that one major racing event per year—the Indy 500 on Memorial Day weekend—was sufficient. Over the years, some of the drivers (Cale Yarborough, Parnelli Jones, Mario Andretti) who have raced Indy cars have also competed in the NASCAR circuit (National Association for Stock Car Automobile Racing). In 1994, NASCAR came to the Speedway oval.

Unlike the sleeker, faster—and possibly more problematic—Indy cars, stock cars have traditionally been driven by the "good ol' boys." Some say stock-car racing began in the 1930s in the South, when bootleggers modified their vehicles in order to outrun the revenuers (excise tax collectors trying to shut down illegal stills during Prohibition). When drivers' informal Sunday afternoon races began drawing crowds, promoters started to sell tickets, and offered prize money to attract better drivers and larger crowds.

The Brickyard 400 Festival involves a week of events held in Indianapolis in early August. A 5-K walk, a 10-K run, a day camp, a racing education program, a celebrity fitness series, a rally and autograph session, and a fairgrounds party lead up to the Brickyard 400 race. Income from the WRTV 6 Do Run Run supports an array of charities throughout central Indiana. Races start in the IUPUI (Indiana University/Purdue University at Indianapolis) natatorium.

Participants in the walk or run pay fees, but spectators can watch the contests at no charge.

During the week before the race, Racing Back to School Camps held in various locations in Indianapolis let children play while learning about racing. The hours vary and admission is free. Indianapolis Life Racing to Fitness, held at the Children's Museum, gives young people a chance to meet sports celebrities while learning about exercise, nutrition, and physical fitness (no admission charge).

Three days before the race, the 400 Festival NASCAR Rally and Autograph Session welcomes the NASCAR racing fraternity with noon-time hoopla in downtown Indianapolis. Party animals will enjoy the Miller Genuine Draft Racefest presented by Q-95 and WRTV (local radio and TV stations) at the Indiana State Fairgrounds. There will be music, a barbecue, and drinks (guess what kind), along with NASCAR show cars, rock music, and interactive entertainment (admission charge). Contact Indy Festivals, Inc. at 317-636-4556.

The Brickyard 400 is a big-money event on the NASCAR Winston Cup circuit, a series of thirty-odd stock-car competitions that begins in February at Daytona Beach, Florida, and ends in November in Atlanta, Georgia. The inaugural Brickyard 400 in 1994 paid out a total purse of over $3.2 million—more than any other NASCAR race in history. **(For race information contact the Indianapolis Motor Speedway at 317-481-8500.)**

At the first Brickyard 400, a NASCAR World 350,000 square-foot theme park debuted on the IUPUI campus. During a four-day period, race fans could watch pit-crew demonstrations, comment on a race (to be taken home on tape), view NASCAR memorabilia, try interactive racing games, pose for pictures with a race car, shop for NASCAR merchandise, and visit concession stands. Two Chameleon units—virtual-reality racing—drew major attention with an interactive adventure ride complete with G-forces and 3-D graphics, simulating stock-car racing at speeds up to 200 mph.

Drivers who raced in the first Brickyard 400 had a wide range of opinions about the experience:

"The Brickyard 400 is just another race on the NASCAR Winston Cup circuit," yawned Mark Martin.

"The Brickyard 400 is the world's premier racing series going to the world's premier racing facility. I haven't been to all that many sacred territories. I've always wanted to go to the Holy Land, and I think Indianapolis is the holy land of auto racing," said Darrell Waltrip.

According to owner Roger Penske, winning the Brickyard 400 has the same effect on a Winston Cup team that winning the Indianapolis 500 does on an Indy car team.

As for food, you can expect to find barbecued chicken, beer, coleslaw, biscuits with honey, veggies with dip, and chocolate cake. Before buying souvenirs, I'd make my way around the NASCAR World theme park and look over the licensed merchandise. Next, I'd count the number of people there, and then I'd consider buying souvenir stock in NASCAR World!

Racing is an important Hoosier tradition. Kids growing up on farms learn to drive on country roads as soon as they can sit on Daddy's lap. As teens, they race one another on isolated roads at night and hope their parents don't hear about it. Kids who grow up in town race from one stop sign to the next intersection. Maybe it's the flatness of the land that encourages speed, or the distant flat horizon. Whatever the reasons, many people here follow racing.

Driver A. J. Foyt, four-time winner at the Indy 500, returned to racing at age fifty-nine just so he could drive in the Brickyard 400. "I would like to be able to say I ran in the first (race), to tell the grandkids," he explained.

As for me, I have four grown sons and three granddaughters. When the first girl was born, we said, "Oh, she's so pretty." When the second girl was born, we said, "She's so smart." When the third girl was born, we all said, "She's going to be a race-car driver!"

There is an admission charge for some events, while others are free. Two-hundred-seventy-five-thousand reserved seats are available in the stands at the Speedway track. **For more information call 317-636-4556 or 800-638-4296.** Visitors to the first Brickyard 400 took whatever hotel rooms they could find anywhere in central Indiana. For help with accommodations, call the Indianapolis City Center 317-237-5206 or 800-468-INDY.

Chesterton Arts and Crafts Fair
Chesterton, Indiana

Children who live near the Indiana Dunes find it easy to dream of living on the beach. After they're grown, they'll be lifeguards or writers or artists and live in a beach house. They'll wake up early and put on swimsuits, then go for a swim in the lake or a walk along the beach, maybe paint a few pictures . . . and in the dream, the money will come.

In the late 1950s, a group of Chicago-area artists who painted at the Indiana Dunes on weekends began holding an annual art fair. They hung their work from two-by-fours, and people came to see it and even to buy. Eventually the artists earned enough money to organize and open the Chesterton Art Gallery.

The Chesterton Arts and Crafts Fair, held each year on the first weekend in August, showcases the work of more than a hundred artists and craftspeople. This strict juried show focuses on fine art and does not involve unrelated activities. Sponsored by the Association of Artists and Craftsmen of Porter County, the festival takes place under canvas in wooded Hawthorne Park, three-quarters of a mile south of US 20 on Waverly Road.

There are three main activities: browsing among the art works created by quality artists, sampling food, and relaxing. Usually there are artists like Judith Birtman from Tallahassee, Florida, with her works in clay; Alex Fong from Oak Ridge, Tennessee, with examples of Chinese paper carving; Marilyn Friece Kelly from South Bend, Indiana, with watercolors; and

Kenneth West from Woodstock, Illinois, with his
works in glass.

Claims Judy Gregurich, executive director of
the Chesterton Art Gallery, "The emphasis is on original art in concept and design." People can browse at
their leisure with none of the modern-day problems
around them.

Concession stands operated by three different
non-profit organizations serve reasonably priced food,
all of which is homemade. Cheese blintzes topped with
real whipped cream are a big favorite, so visit the
Montessori School food booth before they're all gone.
The school also sells treats like couscous salad and
groundnut soup. Other food booths serve Polish
sausage, a turkey-salad plate, Italian beef, popcorn,
yogurt, and so forth. Desserts (the cheese blintzes
were just appetizers) include brownies, cakes, and
Rice Krispies squares.

At the Chesterton Arts and Crafts Fair children
have their own booth, where they can purchase the
materials to make an Art Fair T-shirt, an Art Fair fan,
or other smaller items. The children's booth also has
an adult supervisor, so that parents can relax, knowing
that "their children are becoming the next generation
of artists," says Gregurich.

Your own souvenir might well be an Art Fair
T-shirt or perhaps a favorite craft. Some of the artists
who show here specialize in the Indiana Dunes—maybe
one of them has captured the spirit of shifting sands.

Donations are suggested, and the attendance is usually around ten thousand. **Call 219-926-5645 for more information.**

Chesterton, Portage, Porter, and Valparaiso all have motels and small inns. There are campgrounds at the Indiana Dunes State Park and at various locations in Porter County.

You can choose from several restaurants at the Indian Oak Mall on Indiana Boundary Line Road in Chesterton. Wingfield's has a pub-style dining area and a family room, plus quick service.

Approximately ten miles of Indiana's Lake Michigan shoreline has public access. One way to get to a beach is through the Indiana Dunes State Park (north of Chesterton via State 49). Another is via the Indiana Dunes National Lakeshore, with park sections east and west of the state park.

Octave Chanute, known to some as the father of aviation, found that the windswept Indiana sand hills were just the place for his early flying experiments. Using a flying machine made of cloth, metal, and wire, he made several failed attempts at flight before finally staying aloft for a distance of 487 feet.

For more information, contact the Porter County tourism people at 800-283-TOUR or 219-926-2255.

Columbus Scottish Festival
Columbus, Indiana

Since the 1950s, a small town (population 31,800) in a farming community has acquired a surprising number of buildings designed by architects with well-known names. Throughout the year this community also supports more than fifty events and shows. Whether it's the quilt show in March, Fair on the Square in May, the Scottish Games in July, Chautauqua of the Arts in September, Ethnic Expo in October, or the Festival of Lights parade in December, there are plenty of excuses for visiting Columbus!

The Columbus Scottish Festival, held at the city's Clifty Park each August, celebrates the traditions and heritage of Scotland—especially the games, dances, and music of the Scottish Highlands. Supported by corporate, business, and individual benefactors, the festival offers two days of exhibits, entertainment, re-enactments, and competitions for the entire family.

At one time, until it was repealed in 1782, the British Act of Proscription prohibited the display of anything Scottish. Since then, Scottish culture has re-emerged. Modern Highland games, which may involve fiddle and sheep-dog competitions, music, and dancing, as well as traditional Highland heptathlon events, now take place in Europe, North America, and of course Scotland itself.

"To be a Scot is to be fiercely proud, patriotic, and competitive," claims one Midwesterner with strong Scottish roots. The Highland Games trace their origins back to a time when the Highland chiefs selected the best warriors through a series of competi-

Scots dancers have a fling in Columbus, Indiana.

tions. For safety reasons, modern contests are held with updated equipment. For example, there are modified versions of the caber (tree trunk) throw, the weight toss, the hammer throw, and the sheaf (hay in a jute sack) toss. There are also bagpipe and drumming competitions, and sheep-dog trials. Highland dance competitions include the Highland Fling, the Sword Dance, and another one called "torn trousers" when translated from Gaelic. The ladies dance the Flora and the Lilt, various bands march and play, and it's all quite vivid and colorful. The winner of each contest carries off a trophy.

Just walking around and looking at exhibits can be fun, as is meeting people from different clans. More than two dozen clans and clan societies take part— Buchanans, MacDougalls, McLeods, and so on. Within each clan are many septs—families with different names who are entitled to associate with the clan and wear its tartan. The clan exhibit features family crests, tartans, and other paraphernalia. Scottish vendors have booths selling books, shortbread molds, lace, thistle crafts, patterns, and more.

Since 1992, British cars have been a part of the show, with everything from Rolls-Royce sedans to Morris Minis on display. The lineup of cars on both sides of the entrance provides a twentieth-century welcome.

Stage entertainment takes place at various times on both days. Appalachian folk singer Margaret Gravitt has sung traditional Celtic music at past Columbus Scottish Festivals, and Bob Sander, a storyteller, has performed as well. Re-enactment groups like the 78th Highlanders display uniforms, weapons, and other items typical of the French and Indian War period.

The Parade of Tartans is a high point of the second day, followed by the Wellie Toss and the Bonniest Knees Contest. "It's a time-honored tradition in Scotland for women to throw their men's Wellington boots for fun, exercise, and emphasis," explains one onlooker. So women compete in the Wellie Toss, and the lass with the longest throw wins the contest. Now the knees, of course, will be the most noticeable body part of any Scottish male wearing a kilt; thus, the Bonniest Knees Contest is judged by blindfolded women who choose the best knees using their sense of touch—great fun for all involved.

Adults will enjoy the Ceilidh (pronounced kay-lee) held on Saturday night. This party is much like a traditional Scottish social gathering, with food, dancing, and bagpipe music. (Some guests may even be drinking the "water of life.")

Since 1994 the Youth Scottish Games have been organized for children. There is a Penny Find (pennies are hidden in sandboxes) and a Creation Station, where children can draw, color, or make something resembling their family crest.

The Columbus Scottish Festival has lots of food vendors. Usually one of them specializes in Scottish and British foods like meat pies, "four-for-bridies," and British brands of soda pop.

First thing Sunday morning is the Kirkin o' the Tartan, a traditional Highland church service held on the grounds.

Souvenirs are a cinch to find. The winner of a contest takes home a trophy, and the rest of us go shopping. If you're associated with one of the clans, a crest is ideal. The wooden MacKinnon plaque our family acquired years ago decorates the wall, adds a note

of class, and has lasted a long time—in fact, it has
lasted longer than the marriage!

Admission is charged and attendance is estimated at several thousand. **Call 812-378-2622 or
800-468-6564 for further information.**

At last count the Columbus area had nine hundred and twenty-four hotel and motel rooms. The lux-
urious Columbus Inn (445 Fifth Street) consists of
twenty-nine rooms and five suites in a Romanesque
building that was remodeled at great expense while
keeping the original ceilings, woodwork, and tile
intact. Formerly used as City Hall, the inn is listed on
the National Register of Historic Places. The furnishings are Victorian; there's a breakfast buffet in the
morning and tea in the afternoon.

Other lodging facilities are clustered at the intersection of I-65 and State 46: Holiday Inn, Ramada
Inn, Days Inn, Dollar Inn, Super 8, and so on.

The Empire Tea Room at the previously noted
Columbus Inn welcomes the public for dining.
Zaharako's (329 Washington Street) offers candies,
sodas, and other confections in a 1900 vintage building complete with a mahogany back-bar, onyx soda
fountains, and a Tiffany lamp. (Some of these appurte-
nances date from the St. Louis World Exposition in
1905.) Expect to find Black Cows (root beer with ice
cream), Green Rivers (an old-time soft drink), and
chocolate malts and sodas. You might also ask for a
Tin Roof Sundae (vanilla ice cream, chocolate syrup,
and Spanish peanuts).

Peter's Bay at The Commons—a mall and gathering space designed by prize-winning architect Cesar Pelli—specializes in seafood and also features good steaks, gourmet hamburgers, and salads. Or stop in at the CB, a historic bar that serves soups and sandwiches as well as drinks. Located on Fourth Street across from The Commons, the CB offers a combination of relaxation and sustenance.

One of the reasons for choosing a festival in Columbus is so you'll have a chance to go there! This amazing small town ranks sixth in the nation in the number of contemporary structures (more than fifty) designed by famous architects. Moreover, the higher-ranking communities are all big cities: Chicago, New York, Washington, D.C., San Francisco, and Boston.

In Columbus you'll find examples of the work of Eliel Saarinen, his son Eero, Harry Weese, I. M. Pei, and other talents. They've designed churches, schools, corporate offices, a firehouse, a library, a hospital, and even the county jail.

The Visitors Center (Fifth and Franklin) offers tours of the town's major architectural treasures, including some inside visits (fee charged). Call 812-378-2622 or 800-468-6564. From a vantage point near the center you can see the I. M. Pei library and the Henry Moore sculpture Large Arch, as well as Saarinen's First Christian Church.

The Visitors Center itself is housed in one of about two dozen restored buildings. The Bartholomew County Courthouse (Washington and Third Street) represents the Second Empire style, and the Bartholomew County Historical Society is housed in an Italianate-style former residence (524 Third Street). Two city blocks (800 to 900 Franklin Street) contain various other styles: Queen Anne, American Four Square, Prairie, and Italianate. The Irwin Home and Gardens (608 Fifth Street) was once the home of one of the city's major benefactors.

The Visitors Center has a map with descriptions of these historic buildings for a self-guided tour.

Illinois State Fair
Springfield, Illinois

In the middle of the nineteenth century, fair-goers paid a quarter each for admission to the first Illinois State Fair, and by the third day nearly twenty thousand people had come through the gate at the site on the west side of Springfield. The event featured better methods of farming and raising livestock, along with displays covering labor, industry, education, the arts, and the sciences.

Those early fair-goers should see it now. The bigger and better fair still has its original broad-based appeal, but over the years what was once mainly an agricultural showcase has become much more complex, educational, and entertaining. Recent additions to the long-running Agri-Industries Pavilion and Farm Expo now keep even sophisticated visitors enthralled. There's an exhibit of robotic dinosaurs, a laser light show, and even a chance to try bungee jumping! For a whole lot of good reasons, nearly one million visitors now come to the Illinois State Fair each year. The ten-day event has been held each August at the Illinois

*At the Illinois State Fair kids can
meet calves face to face.*

State Fairgrounds in Springfield, Illinois for more than
a hundred years.

The souvenir program booklet costs about $3.00
and contains a useful map showing where important

things like rest rooms are located on the 366-acre site. Note that the visitor services include sky rides (for an aerial view of the fairgrounds), trams (trackless trains that can be boarded at four different locations), and stroller and wheelchair rentals at the Main Gate and at Gate 2. Note also the location of the lost-and-found children center and the first-aid station. There is even a money machine.

Past fairs have had many fascinating, strange, and zany exhibits, contests, and activities. Illinois has become a leading producer of ethanol, and at the Ethanol Expo you can learn much about this fuel and about the automobiles and tractors designed to use it. The Agri-Industries Pavilion and Farm Expo has a surprising number of active displays, activities for children, and sources of information for consumers. From the grandstand, you can watch horses race around one of the world's fastest one-mile dirt tracks —unless, of course, it's Motorsports Weekend. Then the track becomes a blur of stock cars zooming past at speeds greater than 100 mph. There may also be a mud volleyball contest, a giant sand sculpture, a dare-devil who walks on a moving ferris wheel, or a fashion show for cows!

State fair entertainment—some of it free—has at past fairs included the Beach Boys, Wolfman Jack, Barry Manilow, Salt-N-Pepa, and the Stone Temple Pilots.

The Ethnic Village, a recent innovation in the fair's long history, has become a popular place to eat. You can choose from some fourteen authentic ethnic cuisines, including German, Italian, Polish, Greek, Mexican, and Jamaican. Ethnic Village also has a full schedule of ethnic singers, dancers, music groups, tumblers, and even martial-arts demonstrations.

Children usually gravitate toward Club Mickey D's, where they can play three-on-three basketball or compete in a diaper derby or a smile contest.

There is an admission charge for adults, but children twelve and under are admitted free. Veterans and seniors are also admitted free on special days. A coupon book (if you use all the coupons) reduces each admission charge by half. There is also a charge for parking.

For more information call 217-782-6661 or TDD 217-782-6661.

For dining and lodging information, contact the Greater Springfield Chamber of Commerce at 217-525-1173.

Doll Show and Sale
Archbold, Ohio

I t all began when Erie Sauder—a guy with a woodworking company in Archbold, Ohio—learned that a fifteen-acre farm in the area was up for sale. It had some typical farm buildings on it, along with a barn built by master craftsman George Britsch, so Sauder bought it in 1972. Since then he has acquired other buildings typical of the early nineteenth century and had them hauled from their original locations and reassembled on the Sauder Farm.

As this non-profit living-history complex grew more involved, the operation recruited volunteers to staff the shops, school, church, and other buildings. Now more than a hundred and fifty people dressed in 1860's period clothing help interpret the history of northwestern Ohio at the Sauder Farm and Craft Village.

The Doll Show and Sale, held in August, features two days of doll exhibits and sales accompanied by much "oohing" and "ahhing." A well-known dollmaker or designer usually makes an appearance, and children can make their own dolls from traditional materials such as corn husks, wood, and yarn. The admission price includes a visit to the restored farm and buildings, now arranged as a village on the grounds.

The Doll Show and Sale is only one of many events held at Sauder Farm throughout the season (April through October). There's a quilt show in April (more than three hundred handcrafted quilts on display), gospel music in May, a German Fest in June, Summer on the Farm in July, canning and preserving of food in August, and arts and crafts in September.

Exhibitors come to the doll show from all across the country. To begin with the doll exhibits, head straight for the modern-looking building known as Founder's Hall. Here you'll find booths and tables crammed with all sorts of antique, collectible, and contemporary dolls, along with teddy bears, doll clothes, and accessories. Each year there are thousands of dolls to see, from flouncy ones with faces made of painted china to modern babies made of life-like vinyl. During the 1995 show, doll designer Susan Wakeen created a limited-edition baby doll especially for Sauder Village.

Note that there's usually also a special exhibit of antique dolls, toy bears, or some such in the Greenburg Gallery while the show goes on.

If you haven't been to the village before, take the train ride for an overview. Board the narrow-gauge train at Elmira depot to ride in a semicircle around the buildings and back again. That large metal building from the wrong time period is actually filled with antiques: early washboards, buggies, and crank-start automobiles, and even an early postal truck and fire engine formerly used in the town of Archbold.

A stroll through the village will provide a more detailed view of the way things were in the 1860s. The old general store contains barrels of candy, bright canisters, and a ladder for reaching those glass chimneys on the top shelf. At the wood shop you can watch craftspeople whittling or caning chairs. Down the way, other costumed volunteers might be grinding meal, weaving cloth, or shoeing horses.

Enter the farmhouse to see a typical middle-class dwelling with many antiques. The separate summer kitchen—equipped for preparing, cooking, and canning the family's food—kept the heat out of the main residence. The smokehouse will show you yet another way early residents preserved their food.

The barn, built by a German immigrant named George Britch, holds a mini-zoo of farm animals: horses, cows, sheep, rabbits, and geese. The cackling chickens, enclosed in their coop, already look fat enough for Sunday dinner.

A horse-and-buggy ride offers a change of pace as you bounce along the lane beside a gurgling creek and across a wooden covered bridge. The early doctor's office was brought from nearby Pettisville. The old one-room schoolhouse comes with a teacher in charge, some early desks, and a pot-bellied stove.

Adults will enjoy chatting with the costumed volunteers about the area's early history. Many of the volunteers have retired from other jobs and pursue traditional crafts as hobbies. As with other Ohio attractions, it's strong community support that makes this all happen.

At mealtime, drive two miles down the road to the Barn Restaurant, a huge 1863 building made of hand-hewn timbers. Choose from tables in the hayloft, in the granary, in the dairy section, or even in a horse stall. The waitresses wear period clothing, and the hearty country food gets passed around the table family style. Alternatively, you can fill your plate from the lavish buffet.

Call Sauder Farm (800-590-9755 or 419-446-2541) for more information.

Accommodations are available half a mile from Sauder Village at the Arch Motel (419-445-5541). Two miles away, the new Sauder Heritage Inn combines period styling with high-tech wonders like television sets, coffeemakers, speaker phones, and in-room voice mail. All beds are oversize (kings or queens). Some rooms have balconies, and most open onto an atrium. Reserve a room or a suite through either Sauder Farm number above. For more information about the Archbold area, call 419-445-2222.

South of Sauder Farm via State 66, you can visit the town of Defiance, named for a fort built in the late eighteenth century by frontiersman General Anthony Wayne. It's interesting to note that the land in this part of northwestern Ohio known as Black Swamp was avoided by travelers and settlers alike. Ironically, after the swamp land was drained, farmers discovered that crops flourished in the fertile soil. Tourism information for Greater Defiance can be obtained by calling 800-686-4382.

Swiss Wine Festival

Vevay, Indiana

In mid-August, the folks in Vevay hold a three-day Swiss Wine Festival in their riverside town. Immigrants from Switzerland founded this community early in the nineteenth century, so the event celebrates this heritage with grape stomping, Swiss polka dancers, and beer-and-wine garden dining (no admission charge).

While walking around downtown you can see the home of author Edward Eggleston, the E. P. Schenk house, and the Armstrong Tavern (the oldest building known to have been used as a Masonic lodge). Stay at Captain's Quarters Bed and Breakfast west of town or the at Ogle Haus Inn. **Call the Welcome Center at 800-435-5688 for more information.**

Indian Market

Indianapolis, Indiana

A t the annual Indian Market held at the Eiteljorg Museum in downtown Indianapolis, dozens of talented Native American artists display and sell their weavings, pottery, jewelry, and clothing. Dance and music performances follow each year's creative theme. Located at the corner of West and Washington, the stunning museum was specifically designed to showcase high-quality Native American and Western art. **Call 317-636-9378 for additional information.**

Indiana Avenue Jazz Festival

Indianapolis, Indiana

N ationally-known and locally-appreciated jazz musicians perform at the Indiana Avenue Jazz Festival in celebration of Indianapolis' jazz heritage. The event takes place in the historic Madame Walker Urban Life Center located just a few blocks northwest of city center.

Indianapolis was the 1889 birthplace of jazz musician Noble Sissle. During the thirties, forties, and fifties, Indiana Avenue—now undergoing revitalization —was the site of dozens of jazz clubs. Freddie Hubbard, J. J. Johnson, and Wes and Buddy Montgomery all played here at different times.

The Madame Walker Urban Life Center nourishes this heritage with the annual Indiana Avenue Jazz Festival, as well as with weekly Jazz on the Avenue performances for people who come in after work. **Call the center at 317-236-2099 for details.**

Twins Days Festival
Twinsburg, Ohio

A long time ago, the residents of Twinsburg, Ohio, got used to seeing double. It began when Aaron and Moses Wilcox, identical twin brothers, settled in the community in 1817. About twenty years ago, as part of the town's bicentennial celebration, Twinsburg held a Twins Day festival to honor the Wilcox brothers. Thirty-six sets of twins showed up that year, and since then the word about the Twinsburg festival has spread far and wide. Each year Twins Days, which now lasts three days, attracts about three thousand sets of twins, triplets and quadruplets—both identical and fraternal—and nearly a hundred thousand visitors in all.

Held each year during the first weekend in August at the city park and other sites in Twinsburg, Ohio, Twins Days celebrates life, twinship, and the value of family. In addition to festival-goers, the event attracts research scientists involved in studies of what's been called the largest captive audience of twins anywhere in the world.

At a recent festival the majority of twins attending came from Ohio, while thirty-five percent came from other states, and about one percent from Australia, Hong Kong, Nigeria, Turkey, and Japan, among other nations. Throughout the world, identical twins are born at the rate of one in every two hundred and fifty births; there are perhaps a hundred and twenty-five million individuals who are twins worldwide.

The festival usually tees off with a golf tournament Friday morning, and the afternoon brings field games for children. An outdoor wiener roast welcomes the twins and their families on Friday evening. The Double Take Parade headlines Saturday's activities. Most of the twins walk together near the front, dressed in similar clothing. Others prefer to ride in a hay wagon.

During the course of the weekend, the twins can compete in contests for the most and the least alike, the oldest and the youngest sets of twins, and twins who have traveled the farthest. "Twins have a relationship that's totally unlike other siblings, and this festival is designed to celebrate that," explains Andrew Miller of the Twins Days Festival Committee, Inc. "But . . . there would be no twins without families, and we want to honor them, too."

At noon on Saturday, the twins, their families, and everybody else gather together for a chicken barbecue dinner, followed by entertainment out under a circus tent. Awards are made, and then the thousands of twins (and triplets and quadruplets) crowd onto the hillside for a group photo. Look carefully, and you'll discover that even some of the twins have twins!

The Twin Fireworks helps wrap up a great big Saturday, but there's still more to come. Sunday morning brings a difficult choice between a 5-K Run (proceeds go to benefit Huntington's disease research) and a pancake-and- sausage breakfast. Of course, anyone who finishes the race in time may get in on the breakfast, too. Around 11:00 A.M., an interdenominational church service takes place in an outdoor tent, followed by another chicken barbecue, a twins talent show, and yet another masses-of-twins group photo.

However, "You don't have to be a twin to enjoy Twins Days," insists Andrew Miller. "We invite you to come see what you've been missing. We guarantee a good time."

Plans are underway to develop a Twins Hall of Fame and Museum that will also serve as a permanent location for the festival. Admission is charged, but the registration fee for twins who pre-register is less than the fee for twins who register at the gate. **Call the Twins Days Festival Office (216-425-3652) for more information.**

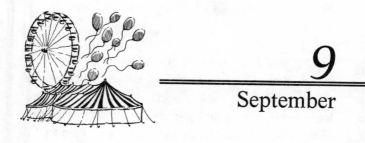

9

September

Mitchell Persimmon Festival

Mitchell, Indiana

"We have the world's best persimmons!" proclaims one town booster. You'll find Mitchell in Southern Indiana about halfway between Indianapolis and New Albany, along the scenic route (State 37). The Mitchell Persimmon Festival takes place during the third week of September, when the fruit is ripe. The local folks, many of whom grow persimmons, have been holding this festival every year since the early 1940s.

Community organizations use the festival to fund various charitable programs, and weekday events take place in scattered locations. During the weekend, Main Street (between Fifth and Eighth Streets) becomes a Persimmon Festival Midway, and there's something for everyone.

Mitchell's long-running Persimmon Festival has become a smorgasbord of things to see and things to eat. Depending on your mood, you can enter a tennis or horseshoe tournament at the city park, drive in the Persimmon Road Rally, go on carnival rides, sing at a community vespers service, dance at the Persimmon Ball, take part in a lip-synch contest, play bingo, enter photos in an amateur contest, or take part in a 5-K walk or run.

If you'd rather just amble around and look at things, that's OK too. There's usually a display of helicopters and emergency equipment organized by the local rescue teams, and you can also watch a parade, view paintings and crafts, tour the nearby Pioneer Village at Spring Mill by candlelight, wander through a huge tent with commercial and industrial displays, see a classic auto show, enjoy gospel singing, and watch the crowning of the Persimmon Festival Queen.

Most of the food stands operate from ten or so in the morning until they run out of food. You'll find chili, ham and beans, cornbread, fried fish, pancakes, breaded tenderloin, and barbecued chicken. Of course, the pièce de résistance of any festival meal will be a dish made with persimmons, whether it's persimmon pudding, torte, cheesecake, dessert roll, pie, cake, cookies, brownies, bread, or ice cream.

For those who don't know (I didn't), the persimmon is native to the entire southeastern part of the United States. The color ranges from orange to black until it ripens between mid-September and late October. The fruit contains too much tannic acid to be eaten without sweetening. Sweetened, canned pulp can be found in gourmet food stores or ordered by mail from Dymple's Delight, Route 4, Box 53, Mitchell, IN 47446-9409.

What do you do with it? Here's persimmon lady Dymple Green's own recipe:

Dymple's Delight Persimmon Pudding
2 cups persimmon pulp and 2 cups sugar
or
1 can Dymple's Delight Persimmon Pulp

2 eggs
1½ cups flour
1 teaspoon baking powder
1 teaspoon cinnamon
1 teaspoon baking soda
1½ cups buttermilk
¼ cup cream
1 tablespoon honey
4 tablespoons melted butter

Mix pulp and sugar or 1 can of persimmon pulp in large mixing bowl. Add two beaten eggs. Add soda to buttermilk and set aside. Mix in dry ingredients, alternating with buttermilk mixture. Add cream and honey. Add melted butter. Pour into 9 x 13 buttered dish and bake at 350 degrees for an hour. Serve with whipped cream topping. Serves 12.

Note that Mitchell's contest for the best persimmon pudding has been running since 1947, and the competition for best persimmon novelty dessert has been running since 1970. Tune your radio to WUME 95.3 FM for complete Persimmon Festival coverage while you're there.

The best adult activity could well be dancing. Choose from the gala Persimmon Ball (semi-formal, over age 21, advance tickets only), square dancing (watch or join in), or a lively rock 'n' roll finale.

Of course, the children will be begging for carnival rides, but take them to kid's day as well (no admission charge). For ages five through twelve they have all sorts of old-fashioned games, with prizes for the winners.

My favorite souvenirs were canned persimmon and a copy of Dymple Green's orange booklet of per-

simmon recipes, which I used together for a tasty
Thanksgiving dessert. For a longer lasting souvenir,
browse through the Mitchell antique shops.

The town of Mitchell grew up around an early
gristmill. Soon grain, meat, and whiskey were being
shipped to places as far away as New Orleans. Unlike
some communities, Mitchell was not passed by when
the railroads came in so it continued to prosper. At the
corner of Brook and Seventh Streets, the restored
opera house—now on the National Register of Historic
Places—offers live entertainment. Instead of the earlier
vaudeville shows, you can now find anything from
bluegrass to pop classics on stage.

When Mitchell resident George James served as
Persimmon Festival Chairman he said, "For you who
are a guest in our city . . . I sincerely hope that you
enjoy every minute of your stay."

While visiting Mitchell I encountered some of the
most courteous, helpful people anywhere. One day,
after trying—and failing—to find a local restaurant
serving persimmon pudding, I stopped a man on the
street. See so-and-so, he advised, pointing me toward a
real-estate office. After the woman inside learned
about my quest for persimmon pudding, she said,
"You need to see Dymple Green." Never mind her
work—she placed the call herself, then handed me the
phone with Dymple (yes, that's her real name) at the
other end of the line.

In minutes I was standing on Green's suburban
lawn in front of a house flanked by persimmon trees.
Throughout this region, it's the people of Mitchell and
other communities who make travel so much fun. **Call**

812-849-4441 for more information about Mitchell and the Persimmon Festival (no admission fee).

Mitchell is located near the intersection of State 37 and State 60. If you can't find a place to stay in Mitchell itself, try the Stonehenge Lodge (fifteen miles north on US 37) or the Spring Mill Inn (a lodge within Spring Mill State Park). You might also call the Chamber of Commerce in nearby Bedford (812-275-4493).

Another local attraction is Spring Mill State Park, just five miles east of Mitchell via State 60. There's a lovely wooded setting with 100 acres of virgin timber, caverns, and an underground stream. Boat trips are available. You can also explore Spring Mill Village, a restored pioneer village with a water-powered gristmill, an old lime kiln, a sawmill, a post office, and other buildings.

The Virgil I. Grissom Memorial Visitors Center contains a space capsule, a video presentation on space exploration, and Grissom memorabilia. A native of Mitchell, Grissom served as command pilot on the first manned flight in NASA's Gemini series. Tragically, he and two other astronauts died in a launch-pad accident in 1967. For more information, call the Greater Mitchell Chamber of Commerce at 812-849-4441.

Madison Chautauqua of the Arts
Madison, Indiana

The picturesque town of Madison grew up as a river port on the north bank of the Ohio River. A large section of the vintage downtown along Main Street has been placed on the National Register of

Historic Places. This historic district remains vital and lively, filled with intriguing shops and stores.

Each year on the fourth weekend in September, the Madison Chautauqua of the Arts holds a juried arts and crafts show with over two hundred exhibitors on an eight-block site. Artists come from all over to exhibit their watercolors, pastels, oils, sculpture, pottery, textiles, works in wood, metalwork, and stained glass all in attractive booths. This show is accompanied by continuous, live folk music played by groups on the Lanier lawn beside the river.

Begin browsing at the James F. D. Lanier State Historic Site (Elm and West First Streets). Completed in 1844, this Greek Revival mansion belonged to a financier who aided Indiana significantly during the Civil War. The arching trees, grassy lawn, and vista of boats and barges that ply the river make a splendid setting.

At special booths for children, young people can practice painting, learn clown tricks, or sing songs. Tunes and foot-tapping melodies waft from a twenty-by-forty-foot tent. Artists may be selling, demonstrating, or discussing their works while browsers and buyers saunter by. Buy something done by a favorite artist as a souvenir.

Later, head east to explore a truly fascinating Main Street. In 1977, Madison was one of three cities among sixty-nine applicants chosen for the Main Street Project of the National Trust of Historic Preservation. Here and there, the historic buildings have become unique shops selling Chautauqua T-shirts and pins, along with framed prints done by local artists. You might also want to consider buying an afghan, since Madison now has its own pattern.

Some of the historic downtown structures have been made into museums open to the public. The Shrewsbury House, Dr. William Hutching's Office and Hospital, the Jefferson County Courthouse and Old Jail, the Fair Play Fire Company No. 1, and the Broadway Fountain are most interesting. The Madison–Jefferson County Public Library was the first library established in the Northwest Territory. Other buildings house appealing restaurants like the Upper Crust, Cafe Camille, Cinnamon Tea Room, Key West Shrimp House, Lacy's on Main, and The Broadway Hotel and Tavern. Still lovely, the spires of Madison's historic churches rise above the tree-lined streets.

If the children get restless, head back to the river to book a carriage ride through the old downtown streets. After that, you can all relax aboard a paddle wheeler named the *Bonnie Belle*. It was river transportation during the early nineteenth century that helped make Madison at one time the largest town in Indiana.

During the late 1980s, the Madison community further developed the riverfront by adding brick walkways and street lamps. Enjoy this setting at mealtime, when booths beside the river offer an impressive array of food: buffalo burgers, cheese, apple cider, fried veggies, fresh roasted nuts, traditional funnel cake—it's all here. Feast at one of the picnic tables beside the river, but save room for the apple dumplings.

For more information, call the Madison Area Convention and Visitors Bureau (812-265-2956) or walk into the Visitors Center at 301 East Main Street.

Free maps with walking tours identify historic buildings. From sixty thousand to eighty thousand visitors come to the Chautauqua of the Arts each year.

Madison sprawls on the wooded Indiana side of the Ohio River. You can drive to Vevay on the scenic highway (State 56) that runs along Main Street and continues east along the river. Swiss immigrants to the Ohio Valley brought rootstock and planted vineyards in this area. In Vevay, the newcomers began making wine in 1802. Ask about tours of nearby wineries.

One mile west of Madison on State 56/62, Clifty Falls State Park has steep cliffs, waterfalls, and hiking trails that range from short and easy to long and rugged. The Clifty Inn (812-265-4135) offers lodging within the park.

Ohio Heritage Days
Mansfield, Ohio

In 1939, Louis Bromfield (1896–1956), a prize-winning author and devout conservationist, built a thirty-two-room home in Richland County in northeastern Ohio. Calling the place Malabar Farm, he used it for entertaining family and friends—many of them celebrities—and for experimenting with various methods of conservation.

In 1976, the Bromfield country estate became Malabar Farm State Park. This scenic 914-acre reserve lies about halfway between Columbus and Cleveland, and twelve miles southeast of Mansfield. In this lovely, rural setting are ponds, hiking and bridle trials, and campsites. Bromfield's Big House, which has been kept just as he left it, is a blend of Western Reserve architectural styles that suggests a gracious past.

Malabar, the name Bromfield chose, refers to a beautiful valley in India. The park service people now caring for the Big House claim they're taking better care of the place than Bromfield did because he let several large dogs have the run of the place.

A tour through Louis Bromfield's sprawling Big House offers a fascinating look at the early lifestyles of the rich and famous. Film stars Lauren Bacall and Humphrey Bogart, known as Baby and Bogey, held their wedding ceremony in the foyer of Bromfield's home.

Ohio Heritage Days, a two-day event held at Malabar Farm State Park, celebrates the rich heritage of rural life in Ohio. Held annually on a Saturday and Sunday at the end of September, this festival offers demonstrations by more than seventy craftspeople in period costumes, exhibits, vintage farm equipment in operation, competitions for draft animals, and entertainment for all.

The main activities take place along a road that loops around the park. Traffic along the circular road moves clockwise. In a smokehouse near Bromfield's house we sampled surprisingly delicious pork that had been smoked at 130 degrees F for thirty-odd hours. Below the road we came upon a huge crafts tent with everything from dolls and quilts to leather goods and metalwork. Anyone too old, too young, or too tired to walk along the road can climb aboard a wagon pulled by draft horses and ride instead.

The festival's sawmill, steam engine, and old gasoline engine demonstrations in another area remind us that people have always invented easier, faster, and cheaper ways of doing whatever they didn't want to do with muscles. Other Ohio Heritage Days demonstrations involve draft-horse competitions (both plowing and pulling contests), the making of sorghum molasses, and assorted pioneer skills. A Civil War encampment and a fur-traders' camp round out the picture of different eras in the state's fascinating history.

On the outdoor stages, various musical groups perform at different times over a two-day period. Country, bluegrass, string bands—each makes a distinctive contribution. Charlie Lewis, Sugar Creek Grass, and the Buckeye Country Cloggers have all played here in the past. On Saturday night, the mood peaks with a square dance in the Main Barn. Join in a do-si-do to the music of Wayne King and the Country Hoedowners or simply watch, clap your hands, and enjoy.

One of the intriguing educational projects housed on this working farm is an herb garden. Adults may enjoy seeing plants similar to those grown by frontier families for use as food or medicine. Spearmint, lemon balm, and yarrow are a few examples.

Children will enjoy the petting farm—located in the working farm complex—where calves, goats, sheep, rabbits, chickens, and other barnyard beasts all run around making appropriate noises. There's also a puppet show on an outdoor stage near the Big House. If the little ones get tired of walking, treat the family to a wagon-ride tour of the farm. A tractor provides the power, and a guide explains the history of the place, so that you can relax while learning about sustainable agriculture.

We found snacks such as coffee, sandwiches, and delicious slices of blueberry pie being sold from booths on the grounds. For a complete meal, the Malabar Inn—a country-style restaurant located on the grounds—serves lunch and dinner from 11:00 a.m. to 8:00 p.m. during Ohio Heritage Days. Call 419-938-5205 for details.

The best places to shop are the craft tent—with its wide selection—and the gift shop in the Louis Bromfield Big House. We saw good-looking shirts, mugs, and postcards, as well as books by Bromfield and by others describing the era when he lived here. **For more information call 419-892-2784.**

Motels in the Mansfield area include Best Western, Holiday Inn, Days Inn, Knight's Inn, and L & K Motel. In the Loudonville area are Little Brown Inn (near town) and Mohican River Lodge (in a remote, woodsy location).

The Kingwood Center on the southwest edge of Mansfield has forty-seven acres of landscaped gardens and woodland hiking trails. Waterbirds swim on the ponds. Greenhouses and gardens have seasonal displays of daffodils, tulips, peonies, roses, chrysanthemums, and other flowers.

Five miles southwest of Loudonville, the Mohican River runs through a forest and a scenic gorge in Mohican State Park. A dam—one of fourteen built by the Muskingum Watershed Conservancy District—forms a reservoir called Pleasant Hill Lake.

For more information about the area call the Tourism Bureau at 419-525-1300 or 800-642-8282.

Valparaiso Popcorn Festival
Valparaiso, Indiana

The parade down Lincolnway features more than a hundred floats, one of which usually carried the Popcorn Royalty: Orville Redenbacher family members and the queen, prince, and princess of the festival. Study the details, and you'll realize that the real king here is popcorn. Popcorn stalks, tassels, cobs, roots, and kernels (popped and unpopped) are used in every float. Two giant corn poppers turn out fresh popcorn all day long for festival crowds. One popcorn executive reported that more than five hundred pounds of popcorn, fifty gallons of oil, and four hundred thousand containers were used in 1990 to feed some eighty-five thousand people.

The Valparaiso Popcorn Festival, with all this popcorn-related hoopla, takes place in northwestern Indiana each year on the Saturday after Labor Day. Festival events occur along Lincolnway, the main street through Valpo's downtown. A hot-air balloon show goes on at the fairgrounds during popcorn festival weekend, and an antique air exhibition draws crowds to the Porter County airport. A week of festival events builds up to the Saturday festival finale.

Scattered yearly events like golf outings, a Popcorn Ball, a Popcorn Festival Queen pageant, a festival Prince and Princess contest, a talent show, a road rally, and foot races for teens take place during the months before the event. Local resident Kathy Brown and

Things are popping in Valparaiso.

other talented local people create the grand float for royalty during the preceding months. Winners of the talent show perform during the festival along with other names.

The activities during the week before change from year to year, but may include Greek Day, Barbecue Chicken Night, breakfast and bingo, finals in the Cutest Baby contest, and road rally awards. Since its inception in 1979, the festival has followed a theme each year, beginning with "A Salute to Orville Redenbacher." Other festivals have been tied to "Popcorn as Fun," or sports, movies, music, holidays, and even the circus.

The Valparaiso Popcorn Festival Parade down Lincolnway is a major part of festival Saturday. Each float that enters is required to use popcorn in at least sixty percent of the float or at least to have a popcorn theme. "People become more creative each year," claims festival director Glennas Kueck. Despite his age, Orville Redenbacher continued to serve as Celebrity Grand Marshall for most Valpo popcorn festivals, beginning with the first event and into the 1990s.

Parking areas for the seventy-five thousand or so visitors, the five hundred arts and crafts vendors, and the sixty-odd food vendors are linked via shuttle transport to the midway. Once you get there, allow plenty of time to stroll from one booth to the next. One major tent honors the town's most famous resident, the late Orville Redenbacher, the familiar face on all those popcorn jars.

With popcorn as its focus, the festival offers all sorts of enticing goodies. Since 1993, festival organizers have chosen certain restaurants to provide lunch in the Orville Redenbacher tent. Other tents and booths sell everything from barbecued pork to egg rolls, as well as vegetables, chili pie, Swedish potato sausage, a variation on Sloppy Joes called "Goopie burgers," and pizza. For those who still want dessert, the fresh caramel corn goes over quite well. So do the elephant ears, funnel cakes, and cheesecake. Several years back, most of the booths ran out of food by mid-afternoon, so you'd better not wait for lunch till 4:00 P.M.!

Adults and teens will enjoy the various entertainers performing on outdoor stages. During past festivals, groups like Five O'Clock Shadow, the Jeff Brown Quartet, Mickey and the Memories, the Devil Dogs, and Kicks have entertained while lots of people danced. There have also been performances by the Northern Indiana Symphony, The Great Pretenders, and the Round Town Ramblers.

While a Popcorn Panic race gives adults a chance to show their stuff, kids get to run in the Lil' Kernel race, held in their own special events area. A kiddie tractor pull also takes place during festival week.

Jars of Orville Redenbacher gourmet popcorn and various other popcorn-related souvenirs can be found everywhere. It's convenient that the festival takes place in Valpo's downtown shopping district, because if the vendors don't have what you want, you can run into a store!

The festival itself is free, but there is a charge for shuttle rides. The number of visitors has leveled off at about seventy-five thousand. **Contact the Valparaiso Popcorn Festival, Inc. at 219-464-8332 or fax them at 219-464-2343.**

The festival sponsors can send you a list of lodgings throughout Porter County, where the event is held. The Carlton Lodge south of town has dozens of rooms, a heated indoor/outdoor pool, and a whirlpool. Other lodging can be found west of town on US 30 near the intersection with I-65.

Within Porter County, the Indian Oak Resort and Spa in Chesterton is pleasantly situated among trees that frame a lake. Behind it, there's a special hideaway, the Gray Goose Inn (219-926-5781). If these rooms have all been taken, look for accommodations at the intersection of Indian Boundary Line Road and State 49.

In Valparaiso, Billy Jack's is a local favorite because of its fresh ingredients and colorful, well-seasoned dishes. Don Quijote (sic), with its Spanish cuisine, also sounds appealing. The Strongbow Inn, southeast of Valpo on US 30, specializes in turkey and offers much more besides.

The Indiana Dunes State Park, thirteen miles north of Valparaiso via State 49, has beaches, hiking trails, picnic grounds, and concession stands. The Indiana Dunes National Lakeshore has sandy beaches located east and west of the state park.

In the artsy village of Chesterton, visit Katie's Ice Cream Parlor for treats after a stroll through the shops in the village.

For more information about lodging, dining, and other attractions, call Porter County Tourism (800-283-TOUR or 219-926-2255).

Penrod Art Fair
Indianapolis, Indiana

P enrod, the largest art fair in the state, takes place on the lovely grounds of the Indianapolis Museum of Art, a cluster of impressive buildings overlooking the White River. About twenty thousand people view the work of two hundred and seventy-five or so fine artists while the Indianapolis Symphony Orchestra, ballet dancing, storytellers, and other groups perform on seven different stages throughout the day. **Contact the Indianapolis Museum of Art at 317-252-9895.**

Ohio River Sternwheel Festival
Marietta, Ohio

E ach year, picturesque stern-wheelers come from upriver and down the weekend after Labor Day to attend a festival held in historic Marietta, home of the American Sternwheel Association. Expect to find concerts, food booths, and relaxed family picnics beside the Ohio River. Saturday usually brings the crowning of a queen, plus varied and continuous entertainment, along with a blaze of fireworks that lights up the flotilla of stern-wheelers and pleasure boats on the water. On Sunday riverside church services are often followed by exciting stern-wheeler races. Admission is free. **Call the Marietta Area Tourist and Convention Bureau (614-373-5178 or 800-288-2577) for more information.**

Jordbruksdagarna (Agricultural Days)
Bishop Hill, Illinois

L ike others who came to America during the nine-teenth century, this group of Swedish people sought freedom of religion. The settlers walked the last hundred and sixty miles across northwestern Illinois to reach a place in Henry County that became known as Bishop Hill. They arrived in 1846 determined to create a utopia on the prairie. During the fifteen years that the early Bishop Hill religious community flourished, around a thousand people came from Sweden to join the colony. The success of this venture encouraged later waves of immigration from Sweden and from Norway and Finland as well.

The Jordbruksdagarna (the word is pronounced yord' brooks doh' gorna and means agricultural days) festival is held each September in Bishop Hill, Illinois. The event commemorates the founding of this village, now a registered historic site. The festival features harvest demonstrations, traditional crafts, games for children, special foods, and hayrack rides.

The festival takes place in a village that is very interesting to explore. Most of the original twenty-one buildings are still standing, and some descendants of the original settlers still reside in the area. There are a restored hotel, a church, a museum, a blacksmith shop, and a village green. Many of the restored buildings are open to the public, and people in period costumes demonstrate tasks from those times.

The nineteenth-century folk artist Olof Krans left a series of paintings that record colony life, and these can be seen in the museum. Krans, who had grown up in the colony, based his paintings of colony people and their seasonal rituals on his childhood memories.

The festival's traditional crafts and skills demonstrations vary from year to year, but everything relates to food or to the harvest. Some of the harvesting during the early years at Bishop Hill was done with a mule team. You may see sorghum, cheese, root beer, or apple cider being made. Displays of mums, pumpkins, and gourds form bright autumn patterns.

Festival food follows the colony traditions. The beefy Bishop Hill Colony stew is always a big hit. Visitors also love the special Swedish rice pudding with grape crumb sauce.

Restaurants at Bishop Hill offer Swedish-American foods in nostalgic settings. Expect Swedish meatballs, open-faced sandwiches, fresh-baked rye bread, and luscious desserts. The Red Oak serves luncheons in a garden courtyard or the Carl Larsson dining room. P. L. Johnson's Dining Room was named for the proprietor of a hardware store that once operated in the building. Antique tables, plants, and decorative lattices provide a cozy atmosphere. Order lunches before 2:00 P.M., and desserts throughout the afternoon. The Bishop Hill Colony Store sells take-home Swedish foods, and the Colony Inn has eat-it-now treats. Olson's Family Tree has a tea room.

Adults will find many excuses to shop here, with nearly two dozen gift shops to choose from. Browse in such shops as Hintze Pottery, Market Day Baskets, The Prairie Workshop, and others. The Village Smithy Gift Shop has vintage quilts. Most of the craftspeople at the festival sell their creations, and many of the early buildings house arts and crafts displays.

Jordbruksdagarna is a family event. Kids will love the hayrack rides, nestled among the bales, jouncing along in horse-drawn wagons. There are other activities and programs just for them. Children may learn about brick-making, for example, or make corn-husk dolls, or enter a corn-shelling competition.

There is no admission charge for the annual Jordbruksdagarna festival, but admission fees or donations are required for the museums. Thousands of people attend. **Contact the Bishop Hill Heritage Association at 309-927-3899 for more information.**

Try Holden's Guest House in Bishop Hill or one of several motels in nearby Geneseo. In Kewanee, which is larger, there are more bed and breakfasts, and additional hotels. If restaurants are crowded, take a carryout picnic to Bishop Hill Park.

The Bishop Hill Heritage Museum has exhibits, books, and information. The museum is in the Steeple Building, located outside the historic site.

Nearby Galva has various antique and crafts stores, a museum, restaurants, and restored older homes. Andover, northwest of Bishop Hill, is the county's oldest community. The Jenny Lind chapel here was endowed by the famous opera singer.

Northeast of Bishop Hill in Johnson Sauk Trail State Park, visit Ryan's Round Barn. Built in 1910 to shelter Dr. Laurence P. Ryan's herd of show cattle, the barn houses a farm museum on the main floor.

Call the Henry County Tourism Council (309-927-3367) for lodging and dining tips. The Western Illinois Tourism Commission (800-232-3889) may also be helpful.

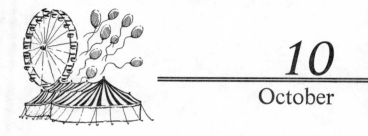

10
October

Feast of the Hunter's Moon
Lafayette, Indiana

Around the Great Lakes about a dozen festivals a
year relate to the legendary Voyageurs. These
hardy adventurers once paddled the waterways hauling
cargoes of food, fabrics, guns, tools, and furs. One
such festival, the Feast of the Hunter's Moon, takes
place beside the Wabash River, known to early Indians
as Ouabache (white water). The feast recreates an
eighteenth-century gathering of French and Indians
about a mile upstream from the site of an early French
trading post. Held in late September or early October
each year, this award-winning event emphasizes
French and Indian cultures during the frontier period.
Sponsored by the Tippecanoe County Historical Society, the feast resembles an early trade fair at which
authentic crafts, food, clothing, and music can be
bought, eaten, observed, and enjoyed.

A major event at the Feast of the Hunter's Moon
is the arrival of the Voyageurs in birch-bark canoes at
the twenty-acre outdoor site. Here and there on the
wooded grounds are Indian tepees and cooking fires,
trading booths, and blanket traders. Visitors and costumed participants mill about each grassy knoll.

Volunteers in authentically designed period clothing demonstrate the traditional metalworking, leather-
working, weaving, doll-making, wood-carving, and

Voyageurs gather for the Feast of the Hunter's Moon.

log-splitting skills used on the eighteenth-century frontier. You can watch the demonstrations and buy lanterns, leather bags, or beadwork while learning more about French and Indian life in North America.

Archeological excavations have uncovered the remains of Fort Ouiatenon (established in 1717)—the first fortified European settlement in this region—downriver from the festival site. There was once a stockade with a double row of about ninety houses around the walls. The French built the fort to keep the British from expanding into this region while they continued their own lucrative trade with the Indians. Over the years the fort changed hands from the French to the British to the Ottawa Indians and back to the French before its final evacuation in 1786. For years, the site was forgotten until archeological excavations began in 1968.

At the re-created feast, costumed volunteers prepare authentic eighteenth-century dishes from natural ingredients for a hungry crowd of thousands. Since the site normally has no running water or electricity, this event is truly from another time. The aromas of sizzling pork chops, buffalo stew, roast corn, and hot, spiced cider draw people to the food booths. More than four dozen types of French and Indian foods fill large tables and simmer in iron kettles over open fires. Operators of the food booths are non-profit organizations that use the proceeds from the event for community projects.

During the feast, performances take place in two arenas and on a rude stage at no extra charge. At various times, puppet shows, French and Indian music, drills, and contests grab the crowd's attention. Late in the afternoon, the traders box up their wares and the musicians pack up their dulcimers. A red-clad fife-and-drum corps halts in front of the blockhouse. The lowering of flags from many nations marks the end of the feast.

The Feast of the Hunter's Moon has long had a no-alcohol policy, and that, plus high standards, superior organization, and extraordinary local support make this a classy event suitable for all ages.

Children can learn how to barter at the children's trade blanket. Using a packet of acorns, buckeyes, and feathers, they can trade for other items. At another booth they can dress up in clothing from earlier periods. They can also watch an eighteenth-century puppet show, make clay pots, and help with bread-making or butter-churning.

Books on crafts and history, as well as children's historical coloring books, can be bought in the Tippecanoe County Historical Association shelter at the east end of the park. Boxes, bags, and baskets of metal, wood, or reed also make great souvenirs. I use such treasures to organize things. Children can buy dolls, drums, tiny leather bags on long cords, and rabbit skins.

Although thousands of people now come to the feast, I sometimes get nostalgic for the early days. Twenty years ago, you could walk up to a working craftsperson and ask questions or snap a photo without dozens of elbows crowding into the frame. At times, the costumed trappers, traders, and craftspeople seem to be enjoying the feast more than the guests.

Be aware that the Feast of the Hunter's Moon takes place at a primitive site during Indiana's typical—i.e., unpredictable—autumn weather. Take along a day bag with rain gear, a jacket, sunscreen, aspirin, tissues, a canteen, and perhaps a woolen throw or shawl. Parking may be half a mile away, so it can be difficult to leave the site and come back again. Consider using the shuttle buses that will take you to and from large parking lots in Lafayette. Let their drivers fight the traffic.

You might also want to visit the Moses Fowler House on a hill on the Lafayette side of the river. Built in 1851 by a leading businessman, the mansion contains historic rooms, exhibits, and galleries and houses the Tippecanoe County Historical Society (909 South Street, Lafayette, Indiana 47901, 317-742-8411).

Seven miles north of Lafayette, at the edge of Battle Ground, you can visit the Tippecanoe Battlefield Memorial. This monument rising from a wooded bluff marks the site of a pivotal battle with Indian forces that helped secure the Indiana territory for European settlers. An interpretive center has a gift shop with handcrafted clothing and books about early history.

North of Battle Ground at the Wolf Park, you can observe several packs of wolves, a herd of bison, some foxes, and coyotes. On Sunday afternoons from May through November, you can watch the wolves test a small herd of bison while you learn more about wolf and bison interaction. Every Friday year-round, there is a Wolf Howl night at which you can learn more about wolf communication. For more information call 317-567-2265.

Call the Greater Lafayette Convention and Visitors Bureau at 317-447-9999 or 800-872-6648 for information about dining and accommodations.

Tuscarawas Valley Fall Foliage Drive
New Philadelphia, Ohio

A country drive on a blue-sky day is one of the great pleasures of a Midwestern autumn. When the sun glows through the October foliage, the leaves take on the brightness of a stained-glass window. About two hours south of Cleveland in the Tuscawaras River Valley, the friendly residents of several sleepy little towns wake up in time to welcome visitors at peak foliage time.

The Southern Tuscarawas Valley Tourist Association Fall Foliage Drive-it-yourself Tour takes place each year on a Saturday and Sunday in early October. Using a map found in local shops and stores, you can begin the tour in New Philadelphia, travel in an easy loop around the southern part of the county, and ends the drive in the historic town of Dennison. You may not travel more than forty miles in a few hours' time, so this is the ideal trip for people who love to stop often along the way.

A leisurely breakfast has nothing to do with the tour, but everything to do with that feeling of well-being that comes from a good meal. I'd head for a place like Randall's Family Restaurant (1013 Front Street SW) in New Philadelphia. They feature the Amish style of cooking (highly caloric) as well as English style (cooking by anyone speaking English rather than Pennsylvania Dutch). You can tell this is a good Amish place, because it opens early enough (7:00 A.M.) to feed the local people. Try their homemade cinnamon rolls, a regional specialty.

Signs of fall in the Tuscarawas Valley.

The drive doesn't actually begin until 11:00 A.M., so if you have time to check out the antiques here, the Riverfront Antique Mall—reportedly Ohio's largest—is just a block away at 1203 Front Street. It's a sprawling eighty-four thousand square feet of space on one floor, filled with the wares of more than three hundred and fifty dealers. After you've walked all over the place, climb into the car for a drive that's short in distance, yet long in memories; journey through scenic countryside at a lovely time of the year.

The route is marked with signs and streamers. You can access the route via State 416 and drive south to the historical marker to learn about David Ziesberger, who came with other Moravian missionaries to settle this area in 1772.

What makes this weekend special are the personal efforts of local people who meet and greet you and even offer refreshments, often without charge. One year Earl Olmestead, author of *Black Coats Among the Delaware,* held an autograph session at the Goshen Cemetery, and a church group made apple butter in the yard of an historic Moravian church on Wainwright Road.

After the antiques-shop owners refresh you with a cold drink, continue on past Wolf and Wolf Station to Table Rock. This sandstone outcropping, formed some two hundred and eighty million years ago, once served as a landmark for travelers passing through. After the area was settled, the rock became a favorite place for picnics and gatherings.

Newcomerstown was once the home of baseball player Cy Young and coach Woody Hayes. The Temperance Tavern, built in 1841, used to shelter travelers overnight. At one time a secret hiding place in the building was used to harbor runaway slaves traveling north via the Underground Railroad. The tavern is now a museum.

During the drive to Port Washington, you'll visit monuments and shops, sample cookies, and get in touch with history. For a time, Port Washington was a stop along the early canal, as well as being a community along Ohio's first state road. The Union Hall, a nineteenth-century building with a steeple like a church, has a unique spiral staircase inside, as well as a display of fire-fighting equipment.

On the way to Gnadenhutten, visit the showroom and factory of American Heritage Hardwoods to see quality country furniture being made. The Lock 17 Mill, a restored gristmill on the canal, now contains craft and specialty shops. The route continues to Gnadenhutten Historical Park and Museum, which features a reconstructed church and cooper's house and the oldest tombstone in Ohio.

Gnadenhutten (which means huts of grace) was settled by a Moravian elder who arrived with a large group of Mohican Indians recently converted to Christianity. The community worked hard and prospered, developing a high standard of living for their frontier location. Tragically, more than ninety of the Christian Indians were massacred by white soldiers in 1782.

The leisurely drive ends in Dennison, where the 1873 Pennsylvania Railroad Depot has been restored. Inside it you'll find a restaurant, an old-time candy counter, a museum, and a gift shop. During World War II, a serviceman's canteen at this site hosted over one and a half million people. The men so appreciated the hospitality of volunteers from miles around that they nicknamed the town "Dreamsville." Between May and December, you can board a train here for an excursion ride.

About two and a half miles east of Dennison on Route 250 there's another antique mall with more than fifty dealers and fifteen thousand square feet of space. The Christmas Tree House, a shop in a renovated 1870's farmhouse, sells imported and handcrafted Christmas items.

There is no charge for the tour, and complimentary refreshments are served along the way. Admission is free to some museums, but donations are encouraged. You get a reduced admission rate at other museums upon presenting your tour map. **Contact the Dennison Railroad Depot (400 Center Street) in Dennison or phone 614-922-6776 for tour information.** You can also call the Tuscarawas Valley Tourist Association (800-527-3387).

New Philadelphia and Dennison each have several motels. Northeast of New Philadelphia via State 39 is the Atwood Lake Resort near Dellroy. Here there are over a hundred guest rooms and several cottages in a wooded lakeside setting. Recreational options include golf, tennis, boating, swimming, and hiking. The dining room overlooks the lake. Call 800-362-6406 for reservations.

Children's Museum Haunted House
Indianapolis, Indiana

As cities grow more crowded, and family time becomes more precious, parents find it difficult to provide the traditional activities that they once enjoyed on Halloween. Designing costumes for children, bobbing for apples, and trick-or-treating can still be fun . . . if and when.

In Indianapolis the Children's Museum Guild creates a Haunted House every year and organizes a
two-week Halloween celebration with the house as a
centerpiece. In addition, they provide special activities
for very young or sensitive children, so that they too
can laugh, chuckle, or squeal instead of bursting into
tears. Created within the Children's Museum and
designed by local artists, the Haunted House involves
walking through a series of rooms designed around an
annual theme such as the Wicked Wild West. Visitors
wander through darkened rooms to discover all sorts
of surprises.

Creators of the Haunted House work with an
electronics company that produces high-tech special
effects, so the Haunted House should thrill you. But
on special days at certain times during the last half of
October, the sponsors offer lights-on visits for children
who would prefer this. During such tours, the Haunted
House is staffed by non-masked characters, and tiny
children will more likely be entertained than frightened.

During the Haunted House show, there's an original Halloween theater production on the museum's
Lilly Theater stage. Especially for children ages two to
six, the performance takes place during the day or
early evening and follows the event's annual theme.
The Children's Museum encourages the entire family
to visit the Haunted House, which began in 1963. An
array of Halloween art activities, contests, and entertainment make everyone welcome.

The festive Halloween spirit leads up to a trick-or-
treat day on October 31. Also held inside the museum,
trick or treat involves special bags, a candy treat, and

tours through the Haunted House. Visitors may tour any time between mid-morning and early evening.

The Children's Museum Guild Haunted House is held during the last half of October each year at the Children's Museum, 3000 North Meridian Street, Indianapolis (admission charge). **Call 317-924-5431 for more information.**

Indianapolis has several dozen hotels and motels to choose from. The Haunted House event takes place about three miles north of the city center. The Radisson Plaza/Suite Hotel, 8787 Keystone Crossing, has family rates and an indoor pool; from it you can walk to restaurants, nightclubs, and upscale shopping, including the Fashion Mall.

Peter's Restaurant and Bar, 8505 Keystone Crossing Boulevard prepares fresh regional dishes in creative ways. Some examples are seared Indiana duckling with fresh berry relish, pepper-crusted pork tenderloin, green bean and bacon hash, and grilled whitefish fillet with light cornmeal crust—need I say more?

Several Laughner's and MCL cafeterias, popular locally, offer an alternative to fast-food chains. Shapiro's restaurant/deli also has cafeteria service at more than one location.

Make sure you allow time to explore the entire Children's Museum, which specializes in natural history, transportation, toys, science, and world cultures. The building has dramatic architecture with multi-levels and clever displays, many of them interactive. There is usually an admission charge, except for one free day a week.

The Indianapolis Zoo, in White River State Park, exhibits animals in simulated natural habitats in a seventy-five-acre area. The enclosed whale and dolphin pavilions are among the world's largest, and various rides and food are available.

Call 800-323-4639 or 317-639-4282 for more information about Indianapolis.

Spoon River Valley Fall Festival

Lewistown, Illinois

Inhabited by early Mound Builders, first settled by Europeans in 1820, and immortalized in *The Spoon River Anthology* by Edgar Lee Masters, the Spoon River Valley with its crafts exhibits, antiques shops, and regional foods makes a lovely drive in any season. During early October, the cottonwood, birch, and maple trees that thrive by the riverbanks glow with autumn color. The local storyteller weaves colorful tales, cloggers dance to the fiddler's tune, and apple butter simmers over the fire.

The Spoon River Valley Fall Festival is a county-wide celebration held in Fulton County, Illinois, during the first two weekends in October. Visitors drive a self-guided, circular route from one town to the next, stopping when they please to peek through the windows of an old schoolhouse or to visit mills that once turned out cloth or to relax in a park with a lovely river view or to try fresh funnel cake.

The entire route loops around the county for a distance of a hundred and forty miles. During the festival, the communities linked by the drive offer special exhibits, foods, and roadside activities. What's more, many activities take place in or near vintage buildings that represent the area's rich history. At London Mills, for example, you can see the Ross Hotel, a typical rural lodging from the early 1900s. At Riverside Park, you might find pioneer-skills demonstrations and get a chance to examine the mill wheels from the town's early days. Middlegrove, Farmington, Avon—each community prepares something special, and you can stop at any number of places: an old coal mine, the site of an early fort, or a railroad museum.

The first mill on the Spoon River was constructed at Ellisville. Since then, this picturesque country village has added an Opera House, an early Christian church (now more than a century old), and what's claimed to be the smallest library in the state. Indians once lived in a village where Mount Pisgah Park is now. Fairview has the oldest Reformed church west of the Allegheny Mountains, and Babylon boasts a distinctive iron bridge.

During the Fall Festival, the Spoon River Valley people prepare traditional foods for visitors to purchase along the way. Expect fresh-baked apple pies, butterfly pork chops, rib-eye steaks, baked potatoes with toppings, onion rings, a local specialty called river fries, and delicious caramel apples!

There's still more ahead—museums, historic mansions, an arboretum, a bandstand, a red brick school, an antiques market, and the first hospital built in Fulton County.

Edgar Lee Masters moved to Lewiston with his family in 1880 at age eleven. After high school graduation, he studied law and eventually became a partner of Clarence Darrow in Chicago. Although many youngsters have grown up reading excerpts from *The Spoon River Anthology*, they may not recall that Masters wrote more than fifty other books during his lifetime. He died in 1950 and was buried in Petersburg (near Springfield), the hometown of his boyhood.

In front of the early Lewistown courthouse Abraham Lincoln gave his powerful "Declaration of Independence" speech against slavery. He restated the principles on which America was founded and insisted that they applied to "all His creatures, to the whole great family of man."

The Fulton County courthouse that was used during the late nineteenth century was burned by an arsonist in 1894. Edgar Lee Masters described this incident in *The Spoon River Anthology*, a collection of stories told by fictional characters who—freed by death—could at last speak their minds. Silas Dement was the arsonist Masters created, and Dement describes his excitement while watching the "glorious bon-fire," formed by the burning courthouse.

The Oak Hill Cemetery in Lewistown, which was familiar to Masters as a youth, became the setting for poetic monologues by two hundred and forty-four spirits who formerly resided in the town Masters called Spoon River. Since the book's publication early in the twentieth century, readers everywhere have valued this telling re-creation of small-town life.

Waterford, site of the first permanent settlement in the county, has many historic buildings such as the Plank Road Toll Booth, the Waterford School from the first settlement, the 1892 Town Hall, and the Spoon River Hotel.

The journey also includes a visit to Dickson Mounds, a branch of the Illinois State Museum and a National Historic Site. This is a rare on-site archaeological museum with excavations, research, exhibits, and interpretive programs about the culture of the region's prehistoric Indians.

The London Mills access to the route can be reached via I-74, State 97, and State 16; another access at Table Grove can be reached via US 136 east of Macomb (no admission charge).

For more information call the Lewistown Chamber of Commerce (309-547-2113) or visit the Information Center, Rasmussen Blacksmith Shop, Main Street, Lewistown, IL 61542.

In Fulton County, Farmington, Canton, Lewistown, and Bushnell have at least one motel per town. Within this county there are also eight campgrounds.

Peoria, nineteen miles east of Farmington, offers Red Roof, Signature, Fairfield, and Holiday Inns, along with Comfort Suites, Pere Marquette, and Jumer's Castle lodges. Call 800-747-0302 or 309-676-0303 for Peoria visitors information.

For dining, Lewiston has five cafes and delis along South Main Street.

At peak foliage time, there are two other ways to enjoy the Spoon River Valley—besides the drive. First, a hiking trail runs through the valley between London

Mills and Lewistown, crossing the river at several points. The second way to explore is by water, in a canoe or small boat. The Indians who once paddled along the Spoon River caught fish and harvested mussels. They used the mussel shells as utensils, or spoons, thus giving the river its name, *Amaquonsippi* (spoon river). Paddlers can go in above or below the dam at Bernadotte. Launch sites include London Mills, Babylon, Ellisville, Bernadotte, Duncan Mills, and Waterford. Named for an early crossing, Waterford is the place where pioneers forded the junction of the Spoon and Illinois Rivers.

Heartland Film Festival
Indianapolis, Indiana

Established in 1992, the Heartland Film Festival recognizes people who make life-affirming films. Crystal Heart awards go to the winners. Held during the last weekend of the month, the festival has film screenings, special events, and workshops. In past years, directors Robert Wise *(West Side Story)* and Sydney Pollack *(The Firm)* and producers Branko Lustig *(Schindler's List)* and Don Hahn *(The Lion King)* have appeared at the festival, held at the historic Madame Walker Theater in Indianapolis. **Contact the Heartland Film Festival at 317-464-9405.**

Ohio Swiss Festival
Sugar Creek, Ohio

Sugar Creek's Ohio Swiss Festival, first held in the early 1950s, has become one of the largest festivals in the state. During a lively two days in October, nearly a quarter of a million enthusiasts converge on this quaint Swiss town in northeastern Ohio. Visitors find a craft show, a festive parade, Swiss-cheese exhibits, polka bands, yodelers, stone throwing, and wrestling.

Located in Ohio's Amish country, Sugar Creek also has lots of cheese shops, bakeries, and gift shops. If you come via horse and buggy (yes, it's possible), there's even a special town parking lot where local buggy drivers tie up their horses! Note that the event takes place on Friday and Saturday, not on Sunday. **Call 216-852-4113 for more festival information.**

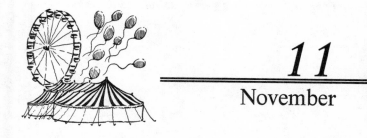

11

November

Christmas In the Village
Waynesville, Ohio

Settlers began building homes in the scenic Little Miami valley late in the eighteenth century. Thus Lebanon, Waynesville, and Morrow grew up along the stagecoach routes that connected Ohio's larger communities. With the harvest chores over and snow on the ground, each annual Christmas celebration meant much to these rural people.

Stroll the brick sidewalks in Waynesville (population 2,000) during the annual Christmas festival to see the gas lamps draped in ribbons and greenery. Dickens characters, strolling musicians, and a town crier pass through the crowd. Visitors ride by in horse-drawn carriages, admiring the shops with their cheery decorations.

Christmas in the Village takes place outdoors each year during the three weekends following Thanksgiving in Waynesville, a small town in southwest Ohio. Known as the "antiques capital of the Midwest," Waynesville becomes even more charming during the holidays. Visitors—some of whom travel across the country to get here—swarm to the Main Street business district, with its thirty-two antiques stores and ten more shops selling gifts or artwork. Many stores operate in restored buildings.

Carolers in Waynesville, Ohio.

The main activity of Christmas in the Village is shopping for gifts in a very festive, welcoming atmosphere. Shopkeepers may offer holiday spiced tea and snacks or free demonstrations of woodcarving, quilting, or weaving. All visitors have to do is smile, browse, and buy.

During the Christmas Walk held on the first festival weekend, Main Street glows with fifteen hundred luminarias (paper bag lanterns.) Visitors may join a procession to a live nativity scene, where actors retell the Christmas story and all sing "Silent Night."

Young children will be thrilled with a ride in a horse-drawn carriage. Older children and adults can have fun guessing the names of the Dickens characters who walk the streets: Charles Dickens himself, his personal secretary George Putnam, the ghost of Jacob Marley, and the notorious Scrooge.

Entertainment includes music performed by a brassy group like Tuba Christmas—a totally tuba band. A guide in a town-crier's costume leads interesting tours.

There are no actual meals provided as part of the festival, but there are several restaurants and cafes on Main Street among the antiques stores, and costumed ladies sell pecan tarts and other delicacies along the sidewalks. The popular Holiday Spiced Tea served by Waynesville shops can be mixed, measured, and stirred—as needed—into a mug of very hot water.

Here's the not-so-secret recipe:
Measure:
1 cup orange-flavored instant breakfast drink powder
$\frac{1}{2}$ cup instant tea powder
$\frac{1}{4}$ cup sweetened apple-flavored drink powder (with spices)
$\frac{1}{4}$ cup sweetened lemonade mix
$\frac{1}{4}$ cup sugar
Combine all the above ingredients in a storage container. Makes $4\frac{1}{2}$ cups of drink mix. Cover with a lid

until ready to make individual servings. For each serving, stir 1 tablespoon mix into a mug of very hot water. Stir till dissolved. Add mix or spices or sugar to taste.

There is no charge for attending the celebration. **Contact Warren County Convention and Visitors Bureau (800-433-1072 or 513-897-8855) for more information.**

Many hotels and motels can be found in the Kings Island–Mason area. The Creekwood Motel in Waynesville has a Main Street location. Waynesville's Hammel House Inn, also on Main Street, has guest rooms in a fully restored 1822 building. The house was once an important stagecoach stop for travelers on the way to Cincinnati or Columbus.

The popular restaurant at the Hammel House Inn is open to the public for tasty lunches that include sandwich creations and a quiche of the day. Der Deutchler, also in Waynesville, serves hearty Pennsylvania Dutch-style meals with much of the food homemade. Expect soups, fresh-baked breads, fried chicken, and mashed potatoes. For dessert, try their traditional milk (custard) pie.

The Golden Lamb, Ohio's oldest inn and restaurant, is located in the nearby town of Lebanon. Expect elegant, traditional, and very high-quality food. The restaurateurs also operate (in Cincinnati) the Maisonette, among the top-rated restaurants in the country.

There are nearly sixty antiques shops in Waynesville, Lebanon, and other villages scattered throughout Warren County, and it's only a fifteen-minute drive (more or less) between one village and the next. Early in December, Lebanon (population 10,000) also has a festive Christmas celebration with a horse-drawn carriage parade. Some fifty thousand visitors come in from everywhere for the winter weekend.

"It's incredible how big this festival has become," says a local businessman.

Many holiday-makers enjoy the excursion train operated by the Indiana and Ohio Scenic Railway between Mason and Lebanon (forty-five minutes each way). During the holiday season, Santa Claus can often be seen lumbering down the aisle, making children wonder, whatever has he done with the reindeer?

International Walkway of Lights
Marion, Indiana

E ach evening from late November into early January, the community of Marion turns on more than two hundred thousand lights in myriad displays that line the river walk between two city parks. Visitors of all ages enjoy driving or walking this two-and-three-quarters-mile route to watch the lights sparkling on the dark Mississinewa River.

Sponsored by Waterfront Festivals, Inc., the International Walkway of Lights begins on the third Saturday of each November and ends on January 2. The route begins at Riverside Park and winds past dozens of lighted, animated displays before reaching the climax—a dazzling white ice castle reflected in Matter Park Pond.

Walk through a candy-cane arch and see animated fifteen-foot-tall toy soldiers salute a welcome. Shepherds watch their flocks, wise men follow a star, and young parents shelter their newborn in a stable. A menorah of lights glows for all.

A suspension bridge stretching two hundred and twenty-seven feet across the river is outlined in lights. A riverboat reminds us that the Indiana territory was settled by passenger and cargo boats traveling on river highways. An animated water mill suggests the water-power once used for grinding meal. Moving horses and an animated stage coach symbolize transport along the early roads.

Besides the array of holiday displays, replicas of world-famous landmarks and thirty-three international flags symbolize the community's multicultural heritage. See if you can recognize San Francisco's Golden Gate Bridge, New York's Statue of Liberty, the Tower of London, the Eiffel Tower from Paris, one of Germany's castles on the Rhine, the Leaning Tower of Pisa (Italy), the great pyramids of Egypt, ancient Mayan temples, or a temple from Japan.

The International Walkway of Lights can be enjoyed by couples out for a romantic stroll or used as a memorable fitness walk or holiday run. If the weather is bad, you can view these displays from a car.

Infants and toddlers bundled in strollers will be entertained by the lights and shifting forms of the riverside scene. During Winterfest—a one-day event that launches this festival of lights—children can enjoy carriage rides, photos with Santa, special crafts for kids, face painting, and storytelling sessions. Along the lighted walkway, children will appreciate the lighted carousel, Santa's elves, a train with moving wheels, and a fantasy toyland.

Everyone can warm up at the end of the walk with hot chocolate and crunchy Christmas cookies. After viewing the wondrous ice-castle finale in Matter Park, head for the gift shop to choose a souvenir from among sweatshirts, Christmas ornaments, stockings, angels, and handcrafted items sold on consignment by local artisans.

There is no admission charged for either Winter-fest or the International Walkway of Lights; however, donations which go to enhance and maintain the light displays can be made in Matter Park. An estimated hundred and fifty thousand people view the riverside displays during the six-week winter season.

The festival can be reached via State 18 west from I-69. You'll find the entrance to Riverside Park (where the walkway of lights begins) near the intersection of State 18 and Nebraska Avenue in the town of Marion. The display runs nightly between 6:00 P.M. and 12:00 MIDNIGHT. There are several motels at State 9, as well as two bed and breakfasts, and several restaurants in Marion.

Other area attractions include the site of the 1812 Battle of Mississinewa at 215 South Adams Street, which is also the location of the Grant County Convention and Visitors Bureau. **Call them at 800-662-9474 or 317-668-5435 for more information about the International Walkway of Lights.**

Christmas In the American Tradition
Columbus, Ohio

Stroll along the boardwalk of this re-created village, and you'll be transported back to the Civil War era. Carolers harmonize in the glow of the nineteenth-century gaslights. Costumed shopkeepers explain the inspirations for their handcrafted shop goods. The traditional holiday foods offered here—inspired by the treats from America's French, German, Irish, Jewish, African, Swedish, and other ethnic groups—can be enjoyed by all.

Christmas in the American Tradition—an annual, month-long festival sponsored by the Ohio Historical Society—takes place at the Ohio Historical Center and in Ohio Village, a reconstructed Civil War-era village on the north side of Columbus. This composite festival celebrates the many traditions that make up America's holiday heritage. There are special opening activities, a shopkeepers festival, town square and Christmas Market activities, and traditional live entertainment. Each component is scheduled at various times and locations within the center and the village during the month.

While Thanksgiving is still a vivid memory, the festival's Grand Opening creates a mood that anticipates Christmas. A Yule log hunt and Christmas tree lighting may well be part of this spirit. The doors and windows of the twenty-two shops and homes in the village are lavishly adorned with greenery, nuts, berries, and other natural materials.

During the first weekend of the event, the Shopkeepers Festival recognizes the merchants who sell quality nineteenth-century crafts such as leatherwork, baskets, period furniture, and Christmas things within the re-created shops. Outdoor vendors also offer sweets and affordable Christmas decorations and novelties at the Christmas Market.

As you move from one building to the next, you could well encounter the Ohio Village Singers in period costumes warbling early American melodies. Or, you might meet a traditional character such as the Dutch St. Nicholas, the Scottish First-Footer, St. Lucia from Sweden, or the German Belsnickel making the rounds. St. Nicholas usually wears knickers and a bearskin cap—he's the one who'll be passing out penny candy.

Entertainment includes concerts by soloists and groups playing dulcimers, fiddles, guitars, Irish pipes, and other traditional instruments. One of the festivals in the past featured the Moravian Trombone Choir and Ellen Ford playing a hammered dulcimer. Candlelight readings are drawn from the work of Charles Dickens and from European and African holiday traditions.

Souvenirs may be found at the Christmas Market or inside the Civil War-era shops. The general store, for example, has favorite old-time toys like Jacob's ladders and paper dolls. Inside the Museum Shop, there'll be cookbooks, children's books, and early novels, as well as jewelry, textiles, baskets, and pottery from various cultures. These are Christmas gifts that represent the American tradition in the broadest sense. You should also look around the museum shop for children's miniatures, like tiny dinosaurs or Civil War soldiers.

The festival food, prepared with a lot of thought, includes various ethnic dishes that reflect Ohio's diverse heritage as well as traditional American treats. There are three ways to dine. The Outdoor Markethouse has sandwiches, snacks, baked goods, and drinks; the most popular items here are roasted chestnuts and wassail, a drink to one's health. Meals are available by reservation only, and dinners are pre-paid. Call 614-297-2606 for more information. The rustic Colonel Crawford Inn (a restaurant that features nineteenth-century fare) offers elaborate buffets; you can also order a dish like turkey breast with fresh sage from the menu of traditional fare. During the festival, the inn's smaller dining room becomes the Victorian Christmas Room, offering lighter and less expensive meals on a first-come, first-served basis.

A great family event, Christmas in the American Tradition offers children's activities much like those of an earlier time. Because young children used to spend leisure time doing school lessons, practicing penmanship, or watching magic shows, today's visiting youngsters may do the same. In the craft workshops, children can make Cathay lanterns or paper decorations just as their great-grandparents did. Children will also enjoy petting the livestock or playing a traditional game called hoops and graces in the village square.

Christmas in the American Tradition begins the day after Thanksgiving and ends just before Christmas. Attendance is about thirty thousand. There is a moderate admission fee for adults and a small charge for older children (children five and under are free). If you make two or more visits during the festival, you'll save money with a season pass. **Call 614-297-2439 for details.**

Hotels and motels are concentrated downtown and clustered around interstate exits. Choose the Radisson Hotel Columbus (I-71 and Morse Road) or the Cross Country Inn (same area) and drive to nearby Ohio Village via I-71.

Looking for special lodging? The Worthington Inn (649 High Street), a renovated historic property from the Victorian era, has a dining room with regional American food, a bar, bellhop service, and individually decorated guest rooms. Call 614-885-2600 for information. Other small inns and bed and breakfasts can be booked through the Greater Columbus Bed and Breakfast Cooperative (614-444-8488).

In addition to Worthington's Dining Room, you can also dine well at Alex's Bistro (Arlington Square Center), Handke's (near German Village), Morton's of Chicago or One Nation (both in Nationwide Plaza), or the Refectory (1092 Bethel Road). For the latest in local favorites, check the "Grumpy Gourmet" column in the *Columbus Dispatch*.

The Ohio Center of Science and Industry (COSI) sounds like an organization that promotes manufacturing, but it's actually a science museum with four floors of interactive exhibits, programs, and demonstrations. The whole family will like it and learn from it. Moreover, there's usually something special for the holidays—perhaps a Christmas tree made with laser light.

The Columbus Zoo (northwest of Columbus via State 257), housed on a 400-acre site beside the Scioto River, has hundreds of species, and over nine thousand specimens in all. This was the birthplace of the first gorilla born in captivity. Take a budding biologist to see the reptile collection and a tiny tot to the Children's Zoo.

For more information, call the Columbus Convention and Visitors Bureau (614-221-CITY or 800-345-4FUN). For more information about the state of Ohio, call the Ohio Division of Travel and Tourism at 800-BUCKEYE.

Huntington Christmas Stroll
Huntington, Indiana

The Huntington Christmas Stroll, held along Fourth Street, features strolling carolers, open houses in various shops, craft bazaars, a cookie walk, and carriage rides. **For date, time, and more information, call 812-683-5065.**

Light-up Corydon
Corydon, Indiana

In the square in Corydon (Indiana's earliest capital), Santa arrives with an entourage clothed in Victorian costumes. Music includes hand-bell choirs, bands, and other ensembles. Enjoy the clamor and the downtown lights while riding around in a horse-drawn carriage. The bell-ringing and the light displays continue into the New Year. **For more information, call the Harrison County Chamber of Commerce at 812-738-2137.**

Nouveau Beaujolais Celebration
Galena, Illinois

T his festive food and wine event is held in the pic-
ture-book riverside town of Galena. Once the
most important city in Illinois, Galena boasts buildings
in a range of nineteenth-century architectural styles,
with about ninety percent of them listed on the
National Register of Historic Places. Galena Cellars
Winery releases its fall wines on this festive weekend,
and music fills the air.

You might see a horse-drawn wagon as it
clip-clops along Main Street delivering bottles of new
wine to shops and restaurants. Friday evening there
could well be a concert and dance, while on Saturday
various restaurants offer special luncheon dishes
accompanied, of course, by the Nouveau Beaujolais.
**For festival information, call 815-777-3330 or
800-397-WINE.**

Buckeye Book Fair
Wooster, Ohio.

B ring in the firewood, pop some corn, and get
ready for those first chill winds of winter with
books, books, books. The Buckeye Book Fair, held on
a Saturday in early November, features more than a
hundred authors and illustrators who live or once
lived in Ohio or have written about Ohio or are
nationally known. Cleveland Amory (columnist and
author based in New York City), Terry Anderson
(who wrote *Den of Lions* about his 2,455 days of captivity in Lebanon), and Helga Sandburg (Ohio poet
whose father was Carl Sandburg) are among the

diverse personalities who have appeared at past festivals to sign books, sell books, and field questions from an admiring crowd of strangers.

Proceeds from the Buckeye Book Fair, a project of *The Wooster Daily Record*, help fund library collections and provide material for literacy programs in the state of Ohio. One recent Buckeye Book Fair raised more than $71,000 for charitable literacy programs throughout the state. What's more, book buyers may purchase intriguing new titles at discount prices.

Held at the Ohio Agricultural Research and Development Center south of Wooster, the fair usually opens at 9:30 A.M. and goes on until 4:00 P.M. At a recent fair, there were more than two hundred and thirty titles for sale, ranging from *Heirloom Recipes* (Marcia Adams) and *Live Your Dreams* (Les Brown) to *Natural Wonders of Ohio* (Janet and Gordon Groene), *Promises to Keep* (Karen Harper), and *It Was Better in the Back Seat* (Sherry Lehman). Admission is free, and more than five thousand people attend. **For more information, call the Wayne County Visitors and Convention Bureau (800-36-AMISH or 216-264-1800).**

Winter Festival, Museum of Science and Industry
Chicago, Illinois

For more than half a century, Chicago's Museum of Science and Industry has celebrated winter holidays with a program that grows broader each year. Formerly called Christmas Around the World, the museum's Winter Festival now includes several celebrations that reflect Chicago's multi-cultural heritage. These holidays of light and enlightenment have led people of different faiths through dark periods: Chinese New Year, Diwali (celebrated by Hindus and Sikhs), Hanukkah, Kwanza (a holiday for African-Americans), Ramadan and Eid-Ul-Fitr (observed by Moslems), and Santa Lucia Day (celebrated by Swedish-Americans). The Holidays of Light exhibit is centered around a huge acrylic sculpture of a flame that illuminates windows representing each holiday.

Winter Festival, which combines the earlier Christmas Around the World and Holidays of Light celebrations, takes place at the Museum of Science and Industry on Chicago's lakefront. Held with the support of the Chicago Park District, the events go on at scheduled times between mid-November and the first of January. On Christmas day, however, the museum is definitely closed.

The popular ethnic exhibits that once formed part of Christmas Around the World continue within the Winter Festival. At last count, the traditions of more than forty countries were shared through tree decorations, holiday songs, seasonal stories, crafts, or plays. During past festivals, the Ukraine, Mexico, the Czech Republic, Denmark, China, Belgium, Serbia, Croatia, Canada, Wales, France, and many other countries were represented. Some countries display authentic ethnic costumes, as well. The museum's Holiday Store offers unique souvenirs, many of them related to the festival theme.

The Museum of Science and Industry, located at 57th Street and Lake Shore Drive, is housed in the last remaining building from the 1893 World's Columbian

Exposition. If you've not seen them before, go down into the Coal Mine or walk through the *U-505* submarine. If you've seen these, then don't miss the museum's newer *Take Flight* commercial aviation exhibit. This one features an actual United Airlines 727 attached to a balcony, a sight that makes people wonder whether the pilot landed here by mistake!

The Holiday Cafe features all kinds of pastries from baklava to apple strudel, plus buttery holiday cookies, good coffee, some sandwiches, and salads. Children have special boxed lunches.

For more information, contact Museum of Science and Industry (312-684-1414). For accommodations and dining in Chicago, contact Chicago Office of Tourism at 312-744-2400 or 800-487-2446.

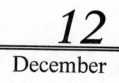

12

December

Christmas In the Dunes

Indiana Dunes National Lakeshore, Indiana

Winters were tough for the early settlers in what is now northwestern Indiana, and only the hardiest survived. In 1882, Joseph Bailly, a fur trader, set up a trading post at a place where the Voyageur canoe route met two Indian trails. He and his wife, who was part Ottawa Indian, raised four daughters in this wilderness among other Ottawas and Potawatomis. Joseph Bailly and his family traded blankets, guns, and cooking pots for beaver, mink, wolf, and other animal pelts and doubtless enjoyed French-Canadian traditions Joseph had known as a child: decorating a Christmas tree, arranging a crèche, hanging stockings, pulling taffy at flirtatious parties, and gathering for holiday feasts.

Christmas in the Dunes, sponsored by the Indiana Dunes National Lakeshore, takes place each year at Bailly Homestead/Chellberg Farm. The celebration combines the French Joyeux Noel at the Bailly home with a Santa Lucia pageant in the Swedish tradition performed by neighbors at Chellberg Farm (half a mile away). Usually held in mid-December on a Sunday afternoon, this festival features traditional customs, food, and folk music in a historic setting now part of the Indiana Dunes National Lakeshore.

In the French tradition, a family would burn a Yule log in their large fireplace on Christmas Eve, saving part of the log each year to burn the following Christmas. Roman Catholic French settlers usually baked a bread called cousins and carried samples around to neighbors while taking up a collection. Moistened wheat placed in a dish in early December foretold good luck if sprouts appeared before Christmas. On Christmas Eve, fresh sprouts were placed in the crèche to make a soft bed for baby Jesus.

Learn more about these and other holiday customs on a visit to the Bailly Homestead, which has five restored buildings from various time periods during the Bailly era: a two-story cabin, a kitchen/chapel, a main house, a brick house, and a fur-trading cabin.

Each year during the festival, volunteers prepare meat pies, ragout (stew), partridge with cabbage, turkey, goose, pea soup, cheese sauce, pickles, and relishes—treats traditionally eaten at the feast that followed midnight mass. There were also desserts such as bread pudding, cornmeal cake, fruitcakes, tarts, ice cream, and wonderful fresh doughnuts.

During Christmas in the Dunes, draft horses with jingle bells pull a huge wooden wagon back and forth between the homestead and the farm. Climb aboard for a ride to Chellberg Farm to learn more about a Swedish Christmas. Here, volunteers use an 1896 wood-burning stove to bake and cook Swedish delicacies. They also prepare traditional art work and entertain with folk music.

The Chellbergs, who once lived on this farm, left Sweden in 1863, made their way to the interior of

Santa Lucia at Chellberg Farm.

North America, and bought forty acres of land from
Joseph Bailly's son-in-law. The seven restored and
reconstructed buildings on view here reveal much
about the lifestyles of three generations of Chellbergs.
The farmhouse, built in 1885 of brick, replaced an earlier frame house that had burned down the year before.

During the festival, a Santa Lucia pageant based on the Swedish legend begins on each half hour between 1:00 P.M. and 4:00 P.M. During a famine in medieval times, it was Lucia who brought food to the hungry in the province of Varmland. Later, during her engagement, she gave away her dowry to the poor. On admitting Christianity, she was accused of witchcraft and burned at the stake. Since then, some people have claimed to see Santa Lucia across a lake, clothed in a white gown and wearing a crown of lights. Today, Santa Lucia represents the spirit of light and hope for all mankind.

Christmas in the Dunes is open to all at no charge. **The festival can be reached via US 20 and Mineral Springs Road. Call 219-926-7561 for more information.**

Note that December temperatures vary near the lake. Be prepared with sweaters, parkas, hats, scarves, gloves or mittens, heavy pants, and boots. Then hope-fully you won't need them! For information about accommodations and dining near the national lakeshore, contact Porter County Tourism at 219-926-2255.

If you're looking for a good restaurant, Phil Smidt's at 1205 North Calumet Avenue in Hammond still offers lake perch and frogs' legs, just as they did back in the 1940s when my father took our family there.

"Try the frogs' legs," he would urge me.

"They taste just like chicken," Mother claimed, as I wondered, "Well then, why can't I just have chicken?"

Phil Smidt's has long since been redecorated and now has a children's menu. Ask whether frogs' legs are on it.

For more tourism information about Lake County dining, lodging, and attractions, phone 219-980-1617 or 800-ALL-LAKE.

Elkhart New Year's Family Fest
Elkhart, Indaina

New Year's Eve in many places has long been linked to a night of carousing. Spend December 31 alone, and you risk a boring evening on the last night of the year. Host a party at home, and you're praying all night that friends won't become obnoxious or bored. Go out to night clubs, and you can spend, spend, spend, without getting much in return. Besides, what will the kids do? Your aging parents? Your rest-less teens?

In 1992, the Elkhart community looked at the holiday New Year's Eve had become and came up with an alternative. Now the Elkhart New Year's Family Fest offers people a low-cost, non-alcoholic celebration with something for everyone. Held each December 31 from 7:00 P.M. to midnight, the event features enter-tainment and refreshments at about ten different downtown locations connected by shuttle bus.

Begin the evening with an upbeat welcome at the Elkhart Civic Plaza and hear a barbershop quartet sing. Move on down to the ELCO Performing Arts Center, and there you'll find a group playing classic rock tunes. Not your kind of music? Then check out

the Chamber of Commerce location, where there's a
string trio playing instead.

By 8:30, a group called the Music Machine may
be pounding out tunes for all the teenagers who gathered earlier at the YM/YWCA. The nachos, pizza, and
hot chocolate for sale will replace the energy they're
burning with their lively talk and dancing. Meanwhile,
the little ones are being creative in the Children's Corner, where storytelling, craft materials, and appropriate
games let them do what they enjoy.

Each site featuring entertainment usually sched-
ules four performances throughout the evening, so you
could watch the magician on the upper level of the
First Congregational Church building four times in a
row. More often, the Family Fest becomes a progres-
sive party, as celebrants board the shuttle to reach yet
another entertainment site. If the child tagging along
with you shows interest in the storytelling, then you
can move along next to the Municipal Building. After
that, your watch says hurry over to the Central Christian Church for the ten o'clock performance of an illu-
sionist—his last for the evening. But you're not
through yet! One of the local hotels is hosting a dance
with big-band sound. Another place has a Dixieland
group called The Chamber Brass playing.

Sandwiches, beverages, and munchies can be
bought at most entertainment sites, and if you make
your way back to the Civic Plaza, there'll be hot drinks
and party hats.

As midnight approaches, everyone gathers at the
plaza for the countdown to the New Year. There might
be a kazoo contest or a sing-along. The mayor shows

up, and the local radio stations broadcast to the stay-at-homes. At the stroke of midnight, fireworks flare overhead, lovers kiss, bells ring, horns blare, and revelers toss confetti everywhere. Those New Year's resolutions will surely wait till morning.

Admission charge covers all events and shuttle transportation, but there are additional charges for most drinks and snacks. Purchasing a Family Fest button allows you entrance to festival sites and use of the shuttle. **For more information, contact the Elkhart County Convention and Visitors Bureau at 800-262-8161 or 219-262-8161.**

A dozen or more motels and motor lodges sur-round the town of Elkhart, and there are more than two thousand rooms available in Elkhart County. The Quality Hotel (300 South Main Street) is conveniently located in the city center (219-295-0280 or 800-221-2222).

Elkhart also has several museums, including Ruthmere, a lavishly restored residence built early in the century, has authentic period furnishings, an elabo-rate player piano, a greenhouse, and an art reference library in the former chauffeur's quarters (302 East Beardsley Avenue).

The S. Ray Miller Foundation Antique Car Museum contains dozens of antique and classic cars, including a 1930 Dusenberg convertible once owned by Al Capone's lawyer. A surprising number of these cars—Cords, Marmons, Studebakers, and Stutzes—were once manufactured in Indiana.

Elkhart County includes many communities of Amish, Mennonite, and other religious groups whose ancestors migrated here to find religious freedom. Nappanee, Goshen, and Middlebury have become trading centers for the Amish; they also have motels and bed and breakfasts.

If you stay at the Checkerberry Inn or at the Patchwork Quilt Country Inn, you'll enjoy great food in on-premises restaurants. South of Elkhart, Come and Dine features country cooking. Amish Acres near Nappanee has a vast restaurant in a barn. Das Dutchman Essenhaus near Middlebury also offers family-style meals.

Call the Elkhart tourism people at 219-262-8161 or 800-262-8161.

Canton Christmas Spectacular
Canton, Ohio

There's something about a live performance that the most sophisticated electronic images will never replace. The sights and sounds of two hundred voices singing Christmas songs in harmony, thirty musicians playing lovely music on various instruments for a range of tastes, soloists, dancers, children, and animals are all right there, so just settle into a comfortable seat and relax.

The Canton Christmas Spectacular, held annually on a four-day weekend early in December, has been called a festival of sight and sound. The massive production, carried out with the help of hundreds of talented residents in the Canton area, features seventy-five thousand lights and different scenes that shift from one century to another.

Held in the restored Canton Palace Theater (605 Market Avenue) in downtown Canton, past Spectaculars have opened with a two-hundred-voice choir singing, an orchestra playing, and ballet dancers coming down the aisles for a production called "Glory to God." "Little Drummer Boy" has followed, with costumed drummers and featured dancers. Popular contemporary music might include "Midnight 'Round the Manger" or "No Eye Had Seen" complete with singers and dancers. Children can take part, too—even children as young as the four-year-olds who once sang a heart-melting "Happy Birthday, Jesus."

As you'd expect, the angels alight on cue with all the right music. Going far beyond the traditional nativity scene with wooden figures, this manger scene *lives*. Joseph and Mary gaze at their newborn. Young shepherds tend flocks of live sheep and lambs. The knowing wise men in striped desert robes—accompanied by a real donkey—humbly present gifts to the Christ Child.

Directed by Larry Wilgus of Larry Wilgus Ministries (an evangelist organization), the Spectacular uses special effects such as photos flashed on a screen; the screen may also provide words when the audience sings the old carols.

The program has variety, the tempo shifts, and there may be jazzy renditions of music like "Rejoice With Exceeding Great Joy." Throughout the evening the Spectacular builds to a grand finale during which chorus, orchestra, and audience fill the theater with selections from Handel's *Messiah*.

Suitable for the entire family, the Spectacular takes place each evening during the long weekend and Saturday and Sunday afternoons. There is an admission charge; ticket sales begin in late October. **Call 216-454-8172 for more information.**

Canton (population 90,000) offers lodging at a range of prices. The Canton Hilton, located downtown, has an indoor pool. Ask about family package rates (216-454-5000).

The downtown Bender's restaurant has old-time tavern décor and a cocktail lounge. Country Manor Family Restaurants (open twenty-four hours), in two locations, have extensive menus and low prices.

Another local attraction is the Pro Football Hall of Fame, which has colorful displays and a large gift shop where visitors can buy mementos of favorite teams.

William McKinley, whose home was in Canton, became the twenty-fifth president of the United States. The McKinley National Memorial, done in beaux-arts style, stands on a rise with a good view of the city. Beside it, the McKinley Museum of History, Science and Industry has interactive displays and exhibits depicting industry in the nineteenth century.

Contact the Canton–Stark County Convention and Visitors' Bureau at 216-454-1439 or 800-533-4302.

Christmas In Zoar

Zoar Village, Ohio

On any ordinary day, the Tuscarawas River flows past a historic village that teems with life as people dine at Zoar Tavern, guests check into an historic inn, and the tinsmith, blacksmith, and dairy workers carry out daily tasks.

As Chrismas approaches, this nineteenth-century community in northeastern Ohio becomes even more appealing as the aroma of gingerbread wafts from ovens, craftspeople in period dress display their handiwork, and a Victorian St. Nicholas ambles down Main Street clothed in long red robes with a garland of ivy around his head. Luminaries line Main Street, carolers sing, and everyone gathers for a tree-lighting ceremony.

The Christmas in Zoar festival, held annually during the first weekend in December, follows a different theme each year. The event takes place in historic Zoar village, where various restored public buildings from an early community become sites for tours, crafts displays, music, a gingerbread-house-building contest, shopping, and dining.

The Christmas in Zoar events usually take place in the Number One House, the magazine complex, the bakery, the Bimeler Museum, the tinshop, and the schoolhouse.

Number One House, the large former residence of the Zoar community leader and two other families, was built in 1835. Specially decorated for the Christmas season, Number One House also has booths for

Christmas in Zoar.

some thirty-five craftspeople who'll show you the textiles or wood carvings or jewelry they've made.

The magazine complex includes the kitchen, the storehouse, and the laundry. All were built during the nineteenth century and restored by the Ohio Historical

Society beginning in 1991. Wander in at festival time, and you may find craftspeople with paintings or wreaths or period furniture.

Horse-drawn wagons take visitors for rides around the village while you move from one building to the next.

In the bakery, Christmas breads, pretzels, or gingerbread may be baking in the brick ovens.

Be sure to view the elaborate gingerbread houses on display in the sewing house. Anyone can enter the Gingerbread House Contest, and prizes are awarded for the three best constructions.

The craftspeople you'll find in the tinshop—a two-room building of brick and timber—follow the tradition of the early tinsmiths who made practical items such as tin cups, buckets, pitchers, and milk pails for the Zoar community.

The 1868 Bimeler Museum was bequeathed to the Ohio Historical Society by a widow who had belonged to the Society of Separatists of Zoar before it disbanded in 1898. Named for the Biblical town in which Lot took refuge during the destruction of Sodom and Gomorrah, Zoar (which means "a sanctuary from evil") thrived from the 1830s until the end of the nineteenth century using a communal system of living. Under the leadership of Joseph Baumeler, an astute businessman, the community at mid-century had assets of about $1 million.

During past festivals, food has been served at the fire station and the Zoar schoolhouse. Organized by a local caterer, the schoolhouse menu has offered cheese sticks, cream-of-broccoli soup, salads, ham-and-cheese croissant sandwiches, beef potpies with puff pastry, baked apples, coffees, teas, hot chocolate, and wassail. The fire station has sold items like sloppy joes, coney dogs, bean soup, doughnuts, and pies.

During past celebrations of Christmas in Zoar, organizers have thoughtfully placed a children's crafts area in the Schoolhouse, where families often dine; there, if children get wiggly, they can work on a craft while their parents finish eating.

Admission is charged, and all proceeds from Christmas in Zoar go toward historic preservation of Zoar village. The Ohio Historical Society sponsors announce the theme of Christmas in Zoar early each year. Special events may change, but the village itself continues to grow as additional buildings are acquired, restored, and opened to the public. Zoar village can be reached via I-77. Take Exit 93 and travel three miles southeast via State 21 to find the festival.

For more festival information call 216-874-3011 or 216-837-3896.

The Zoar Tavern and Inn (One Main Street, Zoar) has five uniquely decorated guest rooms with TVs, phones, radios, and private bathrooms. There is also one suite.

North of Zoar, Canton (population 85,000) has Hampton Inns, Holiday Inns, Knights Inns, and Red Roof Inns, plus Sheraton Inn and Hilton hotels.

Call the Canton–Stark County Convention and Visitors Bureau (800-533-4302) for information about lodging and dining in this area.

Connor Prairie by Candlelight
Indianapolis, Indiana

C onnor Prairie by Candlelight gives people a chance to wander through a restored village by candlelight and pretend it's Christmas Eve in 1836. In Prairietown, costumed docents play different characters and share their opinions about holiday traditions. The candle town features eight nineteenth-century buildings including a doctor's residence, a schoolhouse, and an inn. The event is held at Connor Prairie, a living-history museum located twelve miles north of downtown Indianapolis. **Call 317-776-6000 for details.**

Ethnic Fair
Goshen, Indiana

T he annual Ethnic Fair held on the Goshen College campus celebrates the international background of this community with booths offering traditional ethnic foods, exhibits from dozens of countries, entertainment on three different stages, and an international bazaar with handcrafted items (no admission charge). **Call 219-535-7545 for Ethnic Fair information.**

Mistletoe Ball

Galena, Illinois

C lad in Civil War finery, guests swirl and turn in
time to the music in historic Turner Hall during
the annual Mistletoe Ball. Dancing, socializing with
people from all around the Midwest, and even sneak-
ing an occasional kiss all add to the fun, with the pur-
pose of raising funds for the Galena–Jo Daviess
County Historical Society.

Advance purchase reservations will get you
admission, live music (usually big-band style), hors
d'oeuvres, access to the cash bar, and a chance to
win exciting raffle prizes. Period dress adds to the
fun, but is not required. **For festival information,
call (815) 777-9129.**

Accomodations

Best Western	800-528-1234
Courtyard	800-321-2211
Days Inn	800-325-2525
Doubletree	800-528-0444
Drury Inns	800-325-8300
Embassy Suites	800-362-2779
Exel Inns	800-356-8013
Guest Quarters	800-424-2900
Harley Hotels	800-321-2323
Hilton Hotels	800-445-8667
Holiday Inn	800-465-4329
Howard Johnson	800-654-2000
Hyatt Hotels	800-228-9000
Marriott	800-228-9290
Omni International	800-843-6664
Quality Inn	800-228-5151
Radisson	800-333-3333
Ramada Inn	800-228-2828
Red Roof	800-843-7663
Rodeway	800-228-2000
Sheraton	800-325-3535
Stouffer	800-468-3571
Westin Hotels	800-228-3000

Toll-Free Number Information

USA and Canada	800-555-1212

Tourist Information

Illinois Department of Tourism	800-223-0121
Indiana Travel Information	800-289-6646 or
	800-759-9191
Ohio Travel Information	800-BUCKEYE

Index

A